THE LITTLE BOOK OF
GOLF

DR KEITH SOUTER

ILLUSTRATED BY FIONA McDONALD

*For Andrew, my son and golfing partner. This is for you
with fond memories of the ups, downs and vagaries of this
game that we have shared over the years.*

First published in 2012 by

The History Press
The Mill, Brimscombe Port
Stroud, Gloucestershire, GL5 2QG
www.thehistorypress.co.uk

British Library Cataloguing in Publication Data.
A catalogue record for this book is available from the British Library.

ISBN 978 0 7524 6302 5

Typesetting and origination by The History Press
Printed in Great Britain

CONTENTS

ABOUT THE AUTHOR

Keith Souter was born in St Andrews, the home of golf. He played for the golf second team (when no-one else was available) while he was studying medicine at Dundee University and has had a lifelong love of the sport, collecting clubs and devoting far too much time to a study of the history of the hallowed game. He once won a trophy in a genuine tournament consisting of many eminent golfing doctors and surgeons. It resides on his desk and continually reminds him that golf is more fun than work.

INTRODUCTION

Golf is one of the most popular games in the world. That is a strange thing to say, since almost all serious golfers actually have a love-hate relationship with it. A good round can bring great joy and satisfaction, while a bad round can end in depression, a binge in the bar, arguments with one's partner and the need for prompt evasive action by the family cat.

Golf is unique in that it can be played by people from any age from 3 to 103. It has a unique handicapping system which permits the most abject hacker to play with a top professional in such an even way that they can have a real needle of a match. No other sport offers this.

The fact that people of all ages, all builds and all abilities can play this game may suggest to the untutored that it does not take up much energy, that it is a mere pastime rather than a sport. Say that to a golfer and you risk a verbal tongue-lashing at the very least – people become addicted to golf and as a breed of addict they are incredibly loyal to the game that gives them their fix.

Golf is an equipment sport in which a stationary ball is struck with a variety of clubs. It is played on a large area of land called a golf course, which contains nine or eighteen neatly tended undulating lawns or greens, each of which has a small hole in it measuring exactly 4¼ inches in diameter. The aim is to play each hole in as few shots as possible, and the whole course as near as one can to par or less. Only a minority of players are capable of this. Although this book is written in a light-hearted manner it contains a wealth of information about every aspect of the game of golf. Learn about its long and speckled history and about the early clubs, such as the 'mashie', 'spoon', 'clique' and 'niblick' and see how they developed into the metal-headed 'woods' and 'hybrids' of today. Rejoice in the great names of yesteryear, today and tomorrow. Enjoy finding out about some of the strange things that have happened on links around the world. Read about its strange terminology, its quirks, and the maladies that golfers develop. Find out about strange aberrations like urban golf and read about the different tournaments and the majors of golf, which are the measure by which professionals are evaluated. See also how the game has drifted into literature and films, like a controlled fade that sweeps over the out of bounds and curves neatly back onto the fairway.

For the occasional golfer who finds putting and chipping a total mystery, there are even chapters that may help. Indeed, if the very psychology of the game interests you, there is a chapter on this.

Never was there a Little Book of anything quite so full of it as this one.

1

THE ORIGINS OF GOLF

'Golf is an ineffectual attempt to put an elusive ball into an
obscure hole with implements ill-adapted to the purpose.'
Woodrow Wilson (1856–1922),
28th President of the USA

'IV!'
Ludicrous Golfus (AD 72–101)
(Latin trans: Four!)
[Author's note: Often mistranslated nowadays as 'Fore']

Where did it all start? Golf, I mean.

It really is a curious game, the origins of which seem to be
lost in the distant mists of time. Most people would say that
it started somewhere on the east coast of Scotland, possibly in
St Andrews, that fair grey town in Fife where I was born. This
picturesque old university town is renowned around the world
as the home of golf. With the impressive Royal and Ancient Golf
Club overlooking the Old Course, and with its long tradition
of great champions, nail-biting matches, club-makers on every
street corner and the most knowledgeable caddies touting for
trade in the many hostelries around the town – it just oozes golf.

Such is the esteem in which the venerable old St Andrews golf
club is held that it is known worldwide. It is one of the most
exclusive golf clubs in the world; indeed, more than that, up
until 2004 it was one of the governing bodies in golf. In that year
the responsibility was taken over by a group of companies which
are collectively now known as the R&A – this is the ruling body
for golf all over the world except for the USA and Mexico. That
gives it quite a lot of kudos and most golfers will doff their caps
and accept St Andrews as the home of golf.

Home it may be, yet that does not mean that it is the place where someone first took a bash at a pebble with a stick and launched it towards a hole in the ground some distance off. There are actually a myriad of places dotted about Scotland that could claim to have had the first golf course. Musselburgh, a little town on the Firth of Forth, just 6 miles away from Edinburgh, was established by the Romans and is authenticated by no less an authority than the *Guinness Book of Records* as being the home of the oldest golf course in the world.

There is documentary evidence that golf was being played there back in the seventeenth century. An extract from the account book of Sir John Foulis of Ravelston (1638–1707) – a keen sportsman, lawyer and social historian –records that golf was played as early as 2 March 1632, although apparently Mary, Queen of Scots played there in 1567.

We will keep coming back to this place throughout this book.

THE FIRST KING OF GOLF

King James IV is recorded as being the first Scottish king to have seriously taken up golf when he played at Perth in 1502. That is not the pale Australian imitation, of course, but the real Perth that you come to if you head north from St Andrews. Now King James IV (1473–1513) was an interesting monarch. He came to the throne at the age of 15 and proved himself to be one of the most remarkable of men by anyone's standards. He brought peace to Scotland by beating the heck out of any dissenting nobles on the outer reaches of his kingdom and then he set about educating them. He enforced all landowning families to send their sons to school and then on to one of the three ancient universities of St Andrews, Glasgow or Aberdeen. He was a scholarly monarch and was in fact a dentist.

That's right, that's what I said, he was a dentist. His gracious majesty himself, a King of Scotland actually practised dentistry and surgery. So enamoured was he with the healing arts that he granted a royal seal to the barber-surgeons of Edinburgh in 1506. This Seal of Cause (or charter of principles) stated:

> that no manner of person occupy or practise any points of our said craft of surgery . . . unless he be worthy and expert in all points belonging to the said craft, diligently and expertly examined and admitted by the Maisters of the said craft and that he know Anatomy and the nature and complexion of every member of the human body . . . for every man ocht to know the nature and substance of everything that he works or else he is negligent.

In fact, this seal could almost be a blueprint for the practice of any skill, whether that be dentistry, surgery or golf.

King James IV's grandfather, King James II, who was known behind his back as 'Fiery Face', had actually banned the playing of both golf and football on the Leith Links back in 1457, because it interfered with the practice of archery, which was so important for the defence of the realm. In banning the game, old Fiery Face had said that, 'Golfe be utterly crit doune, and noche usit,' meaning that the game should be cut down and never used or played. You can see that the old boy was no fun-loving sport.

But happily, in 1502 King James IV, the finest of the Stuart dynasty, removed the ban because he no longer saw a threat from England, having just signed a Treaty of Perpetual Peace with King Henry VII. Although he did not know it, it would be several years before Henry VII's son, known to history as bluff King Henry VIII, would start stirring up trouble again.

Some historians believe that one of the main reasons James got rid of the ban was because he had grown tired of dentistry and fancied becoming a golf pro instead. It is doubtful if we will ever discover the truth. As it was, James set off from Scone Palace and bought his first set of golf clubs from a bow-maker in Perth. It is set out in the royal accounts for the year 1502, 'Item: the xxi Sept – to the bowar of Sanct Johnestoun, for golf clubs, xiiii s', which means that he paid 14s to the bow-maker for a set of good clubs; that would be the equivalent of about £350 in today's money, which would be considered something of a bargain. It is hoped, however, that the bow-maker knew that a golf club is ideally made straight, rather than with the shape one associates with a bow.

A SORT OF NOBLE GOLFING CHAPPIE

The year 1457 is the first actual reference on record about the game being played in Scotland, although clearly it had been played regularly before that time. It is likely that old Fiery Face, King James II had been seething about both golf and football for a good few years before he decided to knock both games out of bounds. It may even be that the chap had played a bit himself, only to find that he was a right royal hacker, easily outplayed by those less regal than himself. Perhaps it was royal pique rather than national pride that caused him to blot his copy book as far as golfing history is concerned.

There are, of course, other types of evidence that historians are willing to look at apart from documentary evidence. One such interesting pieces of information is a stained-glass window in Gloucester Cathedral.

This rather beautiful piece of medieval glasswork is hailed by some golfing historians as showing that golf was actually

played in England in the 1340s and the figure depicted has been described as a 'sort of noble golfing chappie driving off.'

This, of course, is complete drivel as an examination by any real golfer (which I hope the reader either is, or aspires to be) will tell you. For one thing the ball is huge – that is no golf ball, I can tell you that. Also, the player is right-handed and has raised his club or stick to his right in readiness to strike the ball that is clearly not stationary. Indeed, the ball is advancing towards him, not departing from a tee, otherwise the depiction would be of the 'chappie' with the club on the other side of his body, or as we say in golf in 'follow through'. And if you are not already convinced, just look at his left foot, clearly that is not the position of a man who has taken up a golf stance, but of someone who has just taken a step in order to thwack a ball hard. No, that is a picture of someone playing a game like hockey, not golf.

A consideration of the history of the 'first golfer' window tells us more. It is situated in the east wing of the cathedral and was commissioned by Sir Thomas Broadstone in 1349, to commemorate his fallen comrades at the Battle of Crécy in 1346, when King Edward III's archers decimated the French army during the Hundred Years' War. This little panel is incongruous even in this context, since it is patently not a battle scene. The suggestion of other historians (mainly French golfing aficionados wanting to claim the game, I suspect) is that it is a depiction of the game of *chole*, which we shall consider shortly.

DOES THE NAME GIVE US A CLUE?

Golf is a strange word; there is no getting away from it. It doesn't sound like an English word at all. So could it be of Scottish origin?

In old Scots the game is called '*gowff*' which actually means 'to strike hard'. That sounds perfectly plausible, but that is all. If that really is the origin, then how did it linguistically get changed to golf? In other words, why the 'l' did it change from that 'w' in the middle?

Howff is a similar word, which means shelter or meeting place. There are still lots of howffs in Scotland that have remained unchanged – should that not have changed as well? That would mean that we should find lots of shelters called 'holf', but we don't, so I suspect that the Scots term gowff, meaning hard strike, thump or drive does not relate to an original term, but is a kind of slang term that was similar to the original word used for the game. This would be in keeping with the fact that there are lots of old Scottish documents that variously describe the game as 'gowff', 'goff', 'gof', 'gouf', 'goif' and 'golve'.

So what are the other contenders? Let's look at them.

Chole

We don't know how old this game is (though it's thought to have been played as long ago as the thirteenth century) but it is still played in southern Belgium. Played by two teams of three players, one team were referred to as the '*chole* players' and the opponents were called the '*decholeurs*'. It was played cross-country with a wooden ball and clubs, the *chole* players having three successive shots to strike the ball as far as possible towards a distant target, which could be a rock, a tree or even the door of a house. Once they had their three shots a *decholeur* player would have one shot to knock the ball as far back as possible, or into an awkward position. Thus the game progressed three shots forward and one shot back for as many shots as was predetermined, or until a score was ratcheted up.

This was not unlike croquet played in the wilds and it has to be a good contender for the original game.

Jeu de mail

This was a more genteel game played on a lawn, not very dissimilar to croquet, which it probably preceded. It is uncertain whether it began in Italy or France, but it became popular in manors, towns and villages where small *jeu de mail* courts would be laid out. It was played with clubs, balls and hoops and existed right up until the French Revolution when all sorts of cuts in sports, sportsmen and even the odd aristocrat were made.

The name, although French, derived from he Latin *malleus*, meaning hammer or mallet.

Pall Mall

This was an anglicised version of *jeu de mail*, which became very fashionable in London in the mid-seventeenth century. It was played on a much larger course than the lawn game that it was derived from. Indeed, the original course was laid out at Pall Mall near St James's Palace. It was later moved to The Mall.

Samuel Pepys wrote in his diary of 1661 that he went: 'To St James's Park where I saw the Duke of York playing at Pelemele, the first time I ever saw the sport.'

Colf or Kolf

The Dutch also have a great claim to being the first to have played a version of golf, and the name that they used, *colf* or *kolf*, certainly sounds convincing.

There is a reference to it having been played as long ago as 1297 in the town of Loenen aan de Vecht, in the province of Utrecht, where a course of four targets was designed and a game played to commemorate the relieving of Kronenburg Castle in

1296. Rather like the Belgian Chole, the targets were not holes, but a door, a windmill, a courthouse and a kitchen.

Curious choices of targets, you may think, but then, everything about golf is curious.

SCOTTISH LINKS

So we come back to Scotland. It does not take a quantum leap to imagine traders from Holland travelling across to the east coast of Scotland and bringing with them the idea of *colf* or even of *chole*. Similarities in the names are tantalising, but even those similarities do not entirely help us, because the origin of those words in the respective languages is not precisely determined. They may have meant clubs or something to do with clubs, rather like the Scots' gowff.

Yet at some point links were set out. We take the word now to simply mean a golf course set out at the seaside and certainly this terrain in Scotland lent itself to a long-distance version of *colf*, *chole* or *jeu de mail*. The rules would almost certainly have been adapted and, since the great outdoors of the Scottish seaside landscape probably had a dearth of windmills, courthouses and the like, some Scottish genius must have thought of the idea of making a hole a target on some sheep-grazed area of grass with a stick to mark it.

We will never know where the first game of golf was played, although there are lots of places, St Andrews included, which would dearly love to have the accolade.

But wait, perhaps there is an ultimate place that maybe we need to look even further back than the medieval period to find. Perhaps back to . . .

THE ROMANS

Yes, the Romans, and why not?

Of course, when you think of sport and the Romans you almost inevitably think of the Colosseum, gladiatorial combat, people being fed to the lions and the odd emperor getting bumped off or playing some instrument or another while Rome burns. That is a gross over-simplification, of course, because the Romans gave us many things: they gave the world mortar, they showed that with enough man-power you can build a straight road over virtually any type of terrain, they devised a legal system that is used by many countries around the world and they gave us mob rule in sport – they were, after all, the original sporting rowdies.

The question is, could they have given us the game of golf as well?

The reason I ask this is because they did in fact play a game with a ball and clubs, called *Paganica*. This had nothing whatever to do with clubbing pagans or throwing balls at them, but was a game played with a leather ball that was stuffed with feathers. Players thwacked these balls at targets with crooked sticks.

Does that sound at all familiar? Of course it does. So this may well have been the origin of the game of golf, especially if they found themselves at the farthest reaches of their empire, in a place like Musselburgh where the lie of the land was just crying out for some enterprising centurions to use their building skills and lay out a links.

Mayhap the Romans who settled in Musselburgh left the world a far greater legacy than they expected?

BUT WHAT ABOUT THE CHINESE?

You may ask, am I serious? The answer is decidedly in the affirmative. The Chinese may well have been playing a game that resembled golf as far back as the Song Dynasty (AD 960–1279). That is the thesis of Professor Ling Hongling of Lanzhou University who has discovered documentary evidence in a book called the *Dongxuan Records,* that shows that this game was played back in AD 945.

His thesis is that golf was invented by the Chinese, then exported to Europe by Mongolian travellers in medieval times, who adapted it to become games like *chole, colf* or *jeu de mail.*

GOLF RULES!

So there you are, it is not at all clear who invented this game. One suspects that people in virtually every country have played games with sticks and balls and frankly I don't really see that it matters who was the first to start thwacking away. It is a bit like trying to work out who invented the bagpipes (we know that the ancient Egyptians, the Greeks and the Romans all played a form of bagpipe, but only the Scots developed the Great Highland Bagpipe).

The thing is, although lots of people played games like golf, it was in Scotland that people started using holes on greens and built up a set of convoluted rules that have grown to be more complicated than any legal system in the world. I propose to leave it at that and conclude that even if they didn't invent the game the Scots deserve to be given credit for being the first to create the organised game of golf.

So there.

Fore!

2

GOLF TIMES

'History is bunk!'
Henry Ford (1863–1947),
founder of the Ford Motor Company

'Hell is a bunker in St Andrews.'
Glen Dullan (I have changed his name to preserve
some sense of dignity for him),
surgeon and rabbit golfer

All great human activities have accumulated a history and golf
has certainly done that, despite the uncertainty of its origins
which we discussed in the last chapter. What follows is a quick
tour through the years, outlining some of the memorable events
that had an impact on the great game.

NOT A GOOD YEAR FOR GOLF – 1457

In 1457 King James II of Scotland (England had to wait until
James VI before they could claim a King James I) banned the
playing of golf because it interfered with the practice of archery,
which was necessary for the defence of the nation.

THE YEAR OF THE FIRST GOLF WIDOW – 1567

Mary, Queen of Scots (1542–87) was the legitimate daughter of King James V. Like her grandfather, King James IV, she liked to venture out on the links. She came in for criticism, however, in 1567 when she went out to play golf after the murder of her husband, Henry Stewart, Lord Darnley. It is not recorded whether it was a good round or not.

SUNDAY CLOSING – 1592

In 1592 the town council of Edinburgh issued a proclamation banning the playing of golf on Sunday, because good people should be listening to the sermons, not gallivanting about enjoying themselves.

Then, in 1610, South Leith Kirk Session suggested that anyone caught playing golf on Sundays should pay a fine of one pound, a substantial fine at that time, which would be paid to the poor. The miscreant golfer would in addition have to confess his sins in church.

YOU CAN DO ANYTHING WHEN YOU ARE A KING

In 1608 King James VI became James I of England and immediately, he had a 7-hole golf course laid out at Blackheath.

In 1618 he proclaimed that golf on Sundays was a good thing after all.

ENOUGH TO SPOIL A GOOD ROUND

In 1641 King Charles I was enjoying a friendly round on the links at Leith when he was informed about a rebellion in Ireland. Some accounts say that he completed the round while others suggest that he excused himself in order to attend to the rebellion. In fact he was relieved to stop because he was not playing well.

A GOLFING MEDICAL STUDENT KEPT A DIARY

Thomas Kincaid, a young medical student at Edinburgh University, kept a diary for the years 1687 and 1688. He was a keen golfer and whenever he could afford the fare, he would set off to the Leith Links to play 'golve'. In his diary he outlined a rudimentary handicap system and gave pointers about how the game should be played.

His entry for 20 January begins:

after dinner I went out to the golve with Hen Leggat. I found that the only way of playing at the golve isto stand as you do at fencing with the small sword, bending your legs a little and holding the muscles of your legs, back and armes exceeding bent or fixd or stiffe, and not at all slackning them in the time you are bringing down the Stroak (which you readily doe).

The ball must be straight before your breast, a little towards the left foot.

THE FIRST INTERNATIONAL MATCH

In 1682 the Duke of York partnered by John Patersone, a cobbler, played two English noblemen at Leith. The Scottish team won and the duke went on to become King James II of England. John Patersone seemed to have been the man of the match, chosen by the duke because of his golfing prowess. At any rate the winning purse was substantial and the duke split it with the cobbler who was able to buy a sizeable house on Canongate on the Royal Mile in Edinburgh. He called the house 'Golfer's Land' and had an escutcheon inscribed on the wall, with the motto 'Far and Sure'.

GOLF IN THE COLONIES

In 1743 a consignment of 96 clubs and 432 balls were shipped out to Charleston, South Carolina.

THE FIRST GOLF CLUB COMPETITION

In 1744 the Honourable Company of Edinburgh Golfers formed the first recognisable golf club and played the first club competition. The prize was a silver club, which was won by John Rattray, the club's first captain.

AND ST ANDREWS FOLLOWED SUIT

In 1754 the St Andrews Society of Golfers was formed. They too had a silver club made and they held their first competition.

In 1764 the St Andrews club decided to reduce its holes from 22 to 18, by amalgamating the first 4 holes into 2.

NEW BEGINNINGS

In 1786 the first golf club in America was formed at South Carolina. There is no record of there having been a permanent course at Harleston's Green, in South Carolina; rather when the golfers decided to play they would dig fresh holes each time and play to them.

In 1829 the first golf club in India was formed with the Calcutta Golf Club. In later years it would become Royal Calcutta.

THE FIRST WOMEN'S COMPETITION

In 1810 a competition was held at Musselburgh for the local fisherwomen.

THE FIRST ROYAL COURSE

In 1833 Perth Golf Club became the first club to be given royal patronage and it became Royal Perth.

THE FIRST PRINTED GOLF BOOK

In 1857 H.B. Farnie wrote *The Golfer's Manual, being an historical and descriptive account of the national game of Scotland*, under the pen name of 'A Keen Hand'.

Henry Brougham Farnie (1836–89) was born and brought up in Fife. He went to St Andrews University and thence to Cambridge before returning to Fife and becoming editor of the *Cupar Gazette*. It was while he was there that he wrote *The Golfer's Manual*, which contained instructions on how to play the game. In 1862 he moved to London and became a successful librettist.

THE OPEN BEGINS

In 1861 the very first Open Championship for both amateurs and professionals was played at Prestwick. The preceding year a championship belt had been played for at Prestwick, which was won by Willie Park. On this first official Open in 1861, Old Tom Morris won the first of his four titles.

In 1870 Young Tom Morris won the title for the third successive year and he was allowed to keep the championship belt.

In 1872 St Andrews, Prestwick and Leith golf clubs provided a silver claret jug as a trophy for the Open. Young Tom Morris won giving him his fourth successive Open title.

AMERICAN CLUBS

In 1884 the Oakhurst Golf Club was formed at White Sulphur Springs in Virginia while in 1888 the St Andrews Golf Club was established at Yonkers in New York. This was followed by Shinnecock Hills Golf Club in Long Island in 1891.

THE US OPEN

This great tournament began in 1895 at the Newport Country Club in Rhode Island.

In 1900, Harry Vardon from Jersey went on an exhibition tour and won the US Open.

FIRST AMATEUR VICTOR

In 1913 Francis Ouimet played 'the greatest game ever' to win the US Open as an amateur.

THE AMERICANS ARE COMING

In 1922 the great Walter Hagen was the first American to win the Open Championship and this signalled the beginning of a period of American dominance.

The amateur golfer Bobby Jones won his first Open in 1926, followed the next year by Hagen again.

THE GRAND SLAM ACHIEVED

Bobby Jones won the grand slam of the time in 1930 and with nothing left to achieve in golf he retired at the age of 28.

And that seems an entirely appropriate point to stop. Don't worry though, there are plenty more snippets of golfing history in the chapters ahead.

3

BALLS

'I regard golf as being an expensive way of playing marbles.'
G.K. Chesterton (1874–1936)

I have to confess that I had a problem deciding in which order to write this chapter and the next. It was a classical chicken and egg question, which came first, the club or the ball? You would imagine that it was the club, or a stick of some sort that some early human picked up and decided to have a whack at hitting a stone. So maybe we should start with the club?

Yet again, which came first, the stick or the stone? There is a good chance that the stone was around before life developed on the planet. In that case shouldn't we start with the ball?

You see what I mean? Philosophical questions can tie you in knots, which is why I think the scientists had the right answer – rather than getting bogged down in matters that could become embarrassingly theological they came up with the idea of the Big Bang. Effectively they said that first of all there was nothing. No matter, no energy, no time. A thing called a singularity occurred and boomf! – or rather, bang! Everything was created. Energy, matter and time, all at once; in one fell swoop they dealt with the chicken and the egg.

I have taken rather the same view and boomf! – I mean, bang – golf was invented, necessitating both some sort of a club and some sort of a projectile, be that a stone or a ball-shaped thing, so we can start with either one. The thing that swayed me, though, was simply that the clubs we use have actually changed and developed as a reaction to each new generation of golf ball that has come along.

So the balls have it! After all, you can't play the game without them, unless you want to be a total fresh air shot specialist.

IN THE BEGINNING THERE WAS WOOD

We actually have no record of anyone playing the game with stone balls or pebbles, unless you count the excellent yarn *The Coming of Gowf* by P.G. Wodehouse as an actual historical record. As we saw in the first chapter the Romans played a game called *Paganica* with leather balls stuffed with feathers. That might have been a forerunner of golf, and if it was then it is true, after the Romans left Britain we really did move into the Dark Ages, socially, culturally and golfically.

It seems likely that golf in the Dark Ages of sport was first of all played with wooden balls. That in itself may mean that it was played in a much smaller area than the golf courses, for wood has a tendency to split. Nonetheless, we do have some ancient balls made of beech and boxwood, both hard woods, which seem to have been used in what was undoubtedly the game of golf in the fifteenth and sixteenth centuries. Indeed, King James VI is said to have used a bowmaker called William Mayne as a supplier of balls.

THE FEATHERIE

The first real advance was made in 1618 when small leather pouches were stuffed with a hatful of chicken, duck or goose feathers. The feathers were boiled and then stuffed into the pouch, which was stitched up into a ball shape and then painted white. Finally, it would be stamped with a special name-punch to indicate that the ball had been produced by the artistry of a particular ball-maker.

As the feathers cooled and dried out they would expand and the leather would contract, to produce a hard little ball that would fairly fly through the air in a far more satisfying manner than a wooden sphere.

They were, however, expensive and fiddly to make and a ball-maker would probably only be able to knock out a half dozen a day. Depending on how well done they were, they would market at half a crown to 5s, which was probably as much as a club.

Two famous featherie ball-makers of the seventeenth century were Andrew Dixon of Leith and Henry Mills of St Andrews. Both towns had, of course, well-known and developed links courses.

THE FEATHERIE WAS IDEAL FOR FAIR WEATHERIE

There were countless problems with the featherie design of course. For one thing, leather absorbs water and they were not great for playing in the damp, which would cause the ball to become heavier, harder to hit and would completely change its flight characteristics.

The other thing of course was that although there was supposed to be a standard way of preparing them – in the early nineteenth century, a top hat full of feathers were used – they could be made however a player instructed the ball-maker. A pebble inside may have given a ball a bit more oomph and it would have been perfectly possible to place a weight slightly off centre to produce a featherie that would fly quite erratically, if it were substituted.

But of course, such gamesmanship, or out-and-out cheating, could never have occurred, could it? Not in a game that was to become the acme of sportsmanship.

Or could it?

One of the great problems about the featherie was its tendency to burst when hit with iron clubs. At that time most clubs were in fact wooden, iron ones only being used in order to extricate oneself from troublesome rough lies. A good thrash with such a club could burst stitching and result in the golfer truly blowing a hole.

A good drive with a featherie would have been 150 and 175 yards.

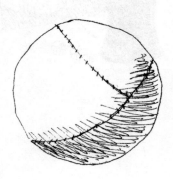

THE GUTTY

The featherie was the golf ball until the 1840s when divine inspiration came to the Reverend Dr Robert Adams Patterson of St Andrews. By all accounts the good reverend was a man interested in all things to do with spirituality, not just his own religion. In 1845 he was unpacking a statuette of the Hindu god Vishnu, which he had ordered from the East, when he noticed that it had been packed with gutta-percha to protect it in its travels.

Gutta-percha (Palachium) is a genus of tropical tree native to south-east Asia and Australia. The sap from the Sapodilla tree produces an inelastic rubber latex and the name gutta-percha comes from the Malay *getah perca*, meaning 'perch sap'.

Anyway, the Reverend Dr Patterson realised that the gutta-percha could be heated in hot water and moulded by rolling into a ball that hardened when cooled. As a golfer he saw the potential and in 1848 invented the gutta-percha golf ball, which became commonly known as 'the gutty'. Here was something that could be produced in quantity and more importantly be produced relatively inexpensively. In addition, a damaged ball could be reheated in hot water then remoulded; effectively, players could renovate their old balls. This was an advance on the featherie which when it burst could only be restitched by an experienced ball-maker or a passing surgeon. Appropriately, the Reverend Dr Patterson's name went down in the annals of golf.

The gutty's flight characteristics were less erratic than the featherie, but as a sphere it could also be quite unpredictable. People found that curiously, once a ball had been played with for a while it would fly more predictably (depending of course, upon the player's technique and ability) and it was realised that the scorings, scrapings and markings actually improved its flight characteristics. A smooth gutty did not travel as far as the old featherie, but after a few games and it was played in, it went further – in any direction. Accordingly, ball-makers experimented by making different types of marks on the ball.

LINES, DOTS AND SPOTS – THEN THE BRAMBLE

The initial trial and error by ball-makers and golfers with various scoring of the surface or etching lines gave way in the 1880s to mass-produced gutties that had regular markings. These were made in moulds, and with Victorian ingenuity, factories were soon churning out heaps of gutties with assorted surface markings.

Criss-cross line patterns were easy to produce and were very popular.

Then along came the spotted ball or, as it was called, 'the Bramble' because it resembled a bramble berry. This was a gutty with tiny raised half-spherical domes all over its surface. It truly revolutionised the game.

And it made big rubber companies like Dunlop a fortune. However, the gutty still had a problem!

Quite simply, because it was a hard, solid ball, it could on occasion smash one of the old fragile wooden clubs, or it could itself explode into smithereens.

AND THEN ALONG CAME BOUNDING BILLIE

The town of Akron, Ohio, played a key role in golf. It was this city that Dr Benjamin Franklin Goodrich, a physician and surgeon who had served in the Union army during the American Civil War, moved to in 1870. There he set up what was to become one of the biggest rubber companies in the country, Goodrich, Tew & Co; it would help to propel Akron into the limelight as the Rubber City.

In Goodrich's day the principal business of the company was to manufacture fire-fighting and garden hoses and bicycle tyres and later they manufactured radial tyres for cars. Sadly Dr Goodrich died at the age of 46, but his company continued to thrive. It was also the background for one of those eureka moments that results in a momentous change for mankind. Well, for that subset of mankind who play golf, at least.

We now move forward to 1898 and enter Coburn Haskell of Cleveland, Ohio, a retired gentleman who was happily enjoying his retirement pottering about on the golf course. One day he went over to Akron to play golf with an old friend, Bertram Work, the superintendent at the F.B. Goodrich Company; the company having changed its name, presumably because one was a company but Tew was a crowd.

Apparently Coburn was in the rubber works waiting for Bertram to get ready when he was idly toying with some rubber thread, winding it to make a ball. Its bounce was unexpectedly high. The actual eureka moment is said to have come on the golf course when Bertram complained to Coburn that he should do something useful instead of frittering his time away; something like invent a decent golf ball that you could hit out of the rough.

The result was that they started work on the development of a ball with a rubber core consisting of wound long strips or threads of rubber. This was then covered in a one-piece outer coat. In 1899 they patented the Haskell ball in the USA and a year later patented it in the UK.

It was a stunning success, flying 20 to 30 yards further than the gutty. Unfortunately, it had more bounce than the gutty, which tended to land on the green and stop after a few small bounces. It was because of this tendency to bound through the greens that it was widely known as 'Bounding Billie'.

Nevertheless, the Haskell ball performed brilliantly for the top players; Walter J. Travis won the USGA Amateur Championship with it in 1901, Sandy Herd won the Open Championship at Hoylake in 1902 and Laurie Auchterlonie won the eighth US Open at Garden City Golf Club in New York.

WAS HASKELL FIRST? – PATENTLY NOT!

In 1904 a legal action was taken by the Haskell Golf Ball Company against Hutchison, Main & Company of Glasgow for patent infringement, after they had produced a range of balls called Springvales. The Scottish company claimed that the patent was invalid because the wound rubber concept had been used by several professional ball-makers since the 1870s. Despite being taken all the way to the House of Lords, the Haskell Company lost.

THE DIMPLE

In 1905 William Taylor introduced the dimple pattern to the Haskell ball. This was the reverse pattern of the gutty bramble, since the dimples were curved inwards while the Bramble had little domes. The dimple made a huge difference to the aerodynamics of the ball and it enhanced the spin so that the ball could be hit higher while the backspin could reduce the amount that the ball would bound.

In the early part of the twentieth century manufacturers kept trying to find the perfect pattern for the cover. A grid pattern called a mesh was taken up and superseded the dimple in popularity for a couple of decades, before being dropped completely when the dimple was chosen as the standard.

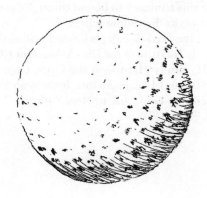

THE PNEUMATIC BALL

In 1906 the pneumatic golf ball was patented. This was essentially a Haskell ball in which a compressed air core – a balloon bag basically – was wound in a huge amount of rubber thread. One of the problems of course, was that the pressure it was subjected to could occasionally cause it to explode when it was very hot!

Manufacturers tried other cores including lead, mercury or cork and there could be marked variations in both size and weight. Accordingly, in 1921 the R&A in Britain and the USGA introduced standard balls that should be used. They were not the same, unfortunately, and players could play with either the British or the American ball. The British was slightly smaller and travelled further, but the American held more spin.

THE MODERN BALL

In 1972 Spalding introduced the first two-piece ball, which they called the Executive. It consisted of a core and a cover and seemed to have better flight characteristics than the pneumatic ball.

Nowadays there is a baffling array of balls, of variable cost. Supposedly they are designed for the different levels of play as indicated by one's playing handicap.

One-piece – this is a solid ball that is pretty useless to play with. It is really just a golf range ball. You certainly know the difference when you hit one of these.

Two piece – this is just a core and a cover, but they travel like heck. They are the balls that will give you maximum distance, but probably minimum spin. They are for the higher handicapper, since they will improve your distance and will have less spin so supposedly they will slice and hook less. The trouble is they also tend to take up less backspin so they are not brilliant for the short game. They usually have a cover made of a hard thermoplastic resin called Surlyn, which is less liable to get cut.

Three-piece – this is the sort for the low single handicap player and the professional. A soft core, possibly semi-liquid, a 'responsive' mantle or middle layer consisting of yards of elastic windings and a cover with good dimples that will enhance the spin. The hacker may cut these. Worse, he may spin them wildly on a slice or hook and lose it in the rough or one of those ponds that acts like a magnet to balls on most courses. They are expensive, so be warned! These may have a Surlyn cover or a softer natural rubber Balata cover. The latter is more liable to get cut, but has better spin quality.

Four-piece – now this is just a show-off ball. Buy them by all means and keep them in your bag, but play with them at your peril if you are not a great striker. They are just like the three-piece, but with an extra mantle layer. Like the three-piece it can have either a Surlyn or a Balata cover.

The four-piece supposedly gives the ball versatility, so that it can be struck with different clubs and will perform well with them all. That is the theory, at any rate. Curiously, that seems to conform with the very purpose of the game, namely to play with one ball and hit it with whatever club was needed.

GOLF BALLS MUST CONFORM TO THE RULES OF GOLF

The R&A and the US PGA, the two governing bodies in golf agree that for a golf ball to be legal it must:

weigh no more than 1.620 ounces or 45.93 grams

have a diameter of not less than 1.680 inches or 42.67 mm

be spherical

conform to initial velocity and overall distance standards

In other words, it has to be fair.

A LITTLE PHYSICS FOR THE NINETEENTH HOLE

Every golfer knows that golf balls fly the way they do because they spin. It was not always the case. At one time golfers thought that spin was bad and that it had to be eliminated at all costs, but then along came physics.

Actually, centuries ago they called it Natural Philosophy rather than physics. Sir Isaac Newton (1643–1727), the great mathematician and natural philosopher who discovered gravity among other things, knew a thing or two about apples and spherical objects. Indeed, in 1672 while watching some fellows play tennis at his Cambridge college he observed that balls curved when they were spinning. In 1852 the German physicist Heinrich Magnus (1802–70) studied this phenomenon and worked out exactly what was happening – it became known as the Magnus effect. Effectively it is a force that is created if a ball is spinning about the axis perpendicular to the flight path.

The Magnus Effect comes into action when a ball is spinning about its vertical axis. That is, a Magnus force will act on a ball spinning clockwise to make it curve to the right (a slice for a right-handed golfer and a hook for a left-hander) while a ball spinning anti-clockwise will have a Magnus Effect pushing it to the left (a hook for a right-handed golfer and a slice for left-hander).

In 1896 the Scottish physicist Professor Peter Guthrie Tait (1831–1901), an enthusiastic amateur golfer, showed how backspin on a golf ball was so important – because of this he can perhaps claim to be the first spin doctor! A mediocre golfer himself, his son Freddie Guthrie Tait excelled at the game, winning the Amateur Championship twice and coming third in the Open in 1896 and 1897.

Backspin on a ball can be explained by the Bernoulli Principle, named after the Dutch-Swiss mathematician and physicist Daniel Bernoulli (1700–82). Essentially, as the velocity of a fluid increases so the pressure exerted by that fluid is reduced. This helps to explain how an aircraft's wings cause it to lift.

Tait showed that a ball spinning about its horizontal axis with the top of the ball coming towards the golfer (i.e. backspinning) will cause an increase in speed of air on top of the ball, resulting in less pressure on top, so the pressure underneath it will lift it up.

*The Magnus Effect
will cause a clockwise-
spinning ball to slice, or an
anticlockwise-spinning ball
to hook*

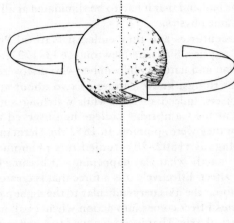

*The Bernoulli Effect
lifts the ball*

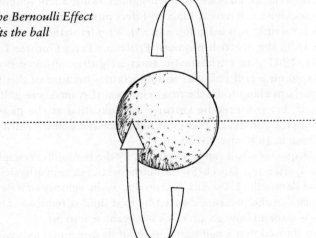

When a backspinning ball hits the ground it will still move forwards until it runs out of forward momentum. If it is still backspinning at that point, the spin will cause it to move backwards until it stops.

In a nutshell the Bernoulli Principle explains how backspin causes a ball to lift while the Magnus Effect explains why sidespin causes a ball to hook or slice.

THE HAPPY NON-HOOKER

There have been various attempts to produce a golf ball that will reduce the tendency to slice or hook. Most infringe the rules laid down by the governing bodies, but they are of interest in terms of physics.

In the 1970s scientists invented the Polara or the Happy Non-Hooker ball which was slightly weighted at the poles of the ball, and which only had dimples on 5 per cent of the surface. The dimples were restricted to the equator of the ball. If the ball was teed up with the dimples in the vertical line then it would tend to fly straight, eliminating 75 per cent of slices and hooks. The principle depended on the dimples providing lift, but the sidewards forces would be reduced. Also there would be the 'spinning dumb-bell rule'. This means that two rigidly connected weights will only spin about one axis at a time.

The Polara range continues to improve. The dimples are all over the ball as they should be, but some are shallower than others, so the underlying principle will and does work. Of course, there is still the way that the ball is struck to be taken into account, which is what golf is all about.

4

CLUBS

'We were all born with webbed feet
and a golf club in our hand here.'
Old Tom Morris (1821–1908),
four times Open Champion

Now I have a confession – I am at heart a traditionalist and a bit of a romantic as far as sport is concerned. In cricket I love the sound of a leather ball on willow. Equally, the satisfying sound of a trusty old wooden driver connecting with the ball is music to my ears. For a while I clung to my woods rather than embracing the new technology until it became abundantly clear that the new 'metal woods' trounced the old woods for both distance and accuracy. It was then that I had my eureka moment.

Well, actually, it was sort of then. I had actually dug out my old squash racquet ready to go off on a short sporting break with the family when it was greeted with howls of derision. It was a wooden racquet, of course, just like the wooden small-headed tennis racquet that they had laughed at the previous summer. And I had to admit, that in both those sports the new technology has transformed the game.

'You are a kind of sporting dinosaur, aren't you, Dad?' Andrew, my son jibed.

Eureka! That was it. I was indeed in danger of going the way of the dinosaurs in sporting terms; I was stuck in time with no hope of progressing. I had to move on. And in my mind I saw that I was one of the lucky ones in golf having lived through amazing changes in the game. I had played with hickory-shafted clubs (not that I was so old, I just inherited them from my father and thought that a proper golfer should use them and I clung to the old names even although everyone referred to the clubs in numerical order), and I had played with both the British and the American balls in my bag when you were still allowed to do so. I realised that my attitude was a bit like me burying my head in a bunker and hoping that no-one would notice me as they played through with their new clubs. Truly I was in danger of becoming an evolutionary blot on the horizon, so in true scientific spirit I decided to adapt and evolve with it.

So I bought some new-fangled metal woods – and they worked. Whenever I go to pick up my golf bag from the half dozen that I have accumulated over the years I hesitate and have to give myself a stern talking to, otherwise I surreptitiously slip one of my antique clubs into the bag. Although the new clubs work better, there is still part of me that hankers for the old days.

THE EARLY CLUBS

In the previous chapter we speculated about whether the ball came before the club. Well, I don't intend going back to the question, except to say that the development of the diversity of clubs used in the game was in part determined by the development of the ball, and in part upon the type of terrain that the game was played upon. Essentially, the old featheries were too expensive and too delicate to be hit at full pelt with iron-headed clubs. Thus the earliest distance clubs were woods with heads made out of hard woods like holly, beech, apple or pear while the shafts were made of ash or hazel. Later hickory became the preferred wood for the shafts, hence it became the generic name for wooden-shafted clubs.

It was only when the gutty came along that iron-headed clubs started to be produced and sought after. Metal heads were made out of iron, which was the most malleable of metals. As we shall see soon, they were all given their own names.

THE ADAM WOOD CLUBS

In 1915 Adam Wood, the captain of Royal Troon Golf Club, donated a set of antique clubs consisting of 6 woods and 2 iron-headed clubs. They are thought to be the oldest set of clubs in existence and experts believe that they may have belonged to one of the Stuart Kings. They were discovered wrapped in newspaper dated 1741 in a boarded up cupboard in a house in Hull and Adam Wood bought them at auction. They are now held in the British Golf Museum in St Andrews, a facsimile set residing in the Troon clubhouse.

THE ORIGINAL SETS

The old golfing terms had a magic about them that has been lost ever since we went numeric. If you have any sense of reverence for the game then you should know the origin of the clubs. After all, they were named with a purpose, even if the sound of them makes you think that they were first coined by a drunken pirate and then modified by the guttural lisp of his aged parrot.

An early set of clubs would consist of the following:

Driver
This is the name that was given to the club used to start the ball off on its journey to the distant hole. In fact in the early days it was called the 'play-club'. The word 'driver' was introduced in H.B. Farnie's book *The Golfer's Manual* in 1857. The term then merely meant the distance clubs, of which there were initially two, the 'play-club' and the 'brassie'.

Brassie
This was originally called the 'grassed driver'. It was used for playing off the fairway and it was given a brass plate underneath to help it cut through the turf and it had a slightly greater loft angle.

The spoon
This was for mid-range and shorter shots. It had a shallow face giving even more loft to lift the ball high. Its name gives the clue; it spooned the ball up in the air and was used for mid-length shots.

Playing a baffing spoon

Baffing spoon

This was another wood that had a smaller head than both the brassie and the spoon. It was used for approach shots and was the forerunner of the iron-headed clubs from 7 iron onwards.

The niblick

This was an iron-headed club with a lot of loft used for pitching the ball onto the green. The name, according to Robert Browning in his excellent book *A History of Golf*, could have been derived from the Gaelic 'neb laigh', meaning 'broken nose', a reference to its shape.

The putting cleek

This was an iron club used to keep the ball low. Originally there were two putters in the set; the putting club for approaching or running the ball up to and onto the green, and a putting cleek used to get the ball into the hole.

THE IRON CLUBS

As I mentioned, once the gutty ball came along then iron-headed clubs gradually replaced the baffing spoon and over time a whole range of other clubs were introduced.

The cleek
This was a relatively thin, straight-faced iron club with just a few degrees of loft, rather like a driving iron or 2 iron. It was used either off the tee or off the fairway for distance shots.

The mashie
This was a mid-iron club that probably revolutionised the game. It was very versatile.

Special clubs
Remember that golf in its early days was played cross-country, so literally any type of lie would be found. Enterprising club-makers made all sorts of clubs, like the 'water mashie', a club with holes in it for hitting out of water or sand.

A water mashie . . .

. . . and how you use it.

Or there was the 'rutting club' (I know, it sounds rude), which actually had nothing to do with testosterone-heavy stags, but was a narrow little club used for getting out of cart ruts.

There was also a 'jigger', used to make the ball jig up to the hole. This was a sort of runner-up club.

The whole range of hickory clubs and their modern counterparts:

Hickory	Angle of loft (approximate)	Modern
Play club	8–12°	Driver
Grassed driver or brassie	12–14°	2 wood
Spoon	15–18°	3 wood
Baffing spoon	25–35°	7 wood

Iron-headed hickories:

Cleek	17–19°	1 or 2 iron
Mid-mashie	20°	3 iron
Mashie-iron	23°	4 iron
Mashie	26–30°	5 iron
Spade-mashie	30–32°	6 iron
Mashie-niblick	34°	7 iron
Pitching niblick or lofting iron	38°	8 iron
Niblick	40–5°	9 iron
Putting cleek	0°	putter

Please note – these are only approximations! The early club-makers made things by hand and by feel, therefore there was terrific overlap in clubs. I am well aware that there are many listings of clubs that have been made, and some will be different to this. So I won't worry about it and neither should you, gentle reader.

SABBATH STICKS

As you may recollect from chapter 1, old Fiery Face King James II banned golf since it was interfering with archery practice. In later days the playing of the game was permitted, but the Church of Scotland frowned upon it being played on Sundays. Indeed, in 1593 John Henrie and Pat Rogie were jailed in Edinburgh for playing golf at Leith when they should have been in church listening to a sermon about the evils of golf.

As the saying goes, desperate times demand desperate measures and enterprising club-makers started making Sabbath sticks, clubs fashioned as walking-sticks with the clubhead small enough to be held in the hand. When no-one was looking a desperate golfer could put down a featherie and play on his way to the kirk.

HICKORY DICKORY

After the First World War there was a shortage of hickory and golf club manufacturers started experimenting with steel shafts. Hollow tubes proved to be far superior to hickory and the game leaped forwards again.

Grooves became standardised and were found to be far more efficient than the old dot depressions that the club-makers used to hammer onto the faces.

New technology introduced lighter materials and in 1973 graphite shafts were developed and permitted. Science was introduced and the shape of clubheads, their weighting and their angulations moved to ever greater levels. Now, some people question whether the technology is going too far, permitting the ball to be struck farther and straighter than ever before; interesting questions, but I suspect that most golfers would like to be able to hit the ball a country mile.

DID YOU KNOW?

Golf bags started to be used in the 1880s. Up until then a caddie just carried a collection under his arm.

HOW MANY CLUBS?

Up until 1939 you could carry as many clubs as you wanted. Francis Ouimet won the 1913 US Open with only 7 clubs while in 1934 the Amateur Championship was won by Lawson Little with 31 clubs. In 1939 the rules were changed so that a player is only permitted 14 clubs.

THE BIGGEST DRIVER IN THE WORLD

I told you that I am a traditionalist in golf, yet I also have to admit to having as big a gullible streak as the next player. I buy all the latest gimmicks, clubs, instructional videos and golf magazines – I see, I read, I buy and I try out all the panaceas that will marvellously transform the utter jack rabbit into a sleek tiger. Over the years I have bought wonder clubs that they say will allow you to dispense with twelve clubs in the bag, short irons that will get you out of trouble from anywhere between 250 yards to 20ft from the hole, and clubs with impossibly high lofts that will enable you to lob a shot over an oak tree when you are virtually standing under it.

The world's biggest driver was one such club; it promised to have the biggest head, the largest sweet spot and a shaft specially designed so that it counteracted hooks, slices and foozles. It would amaze you and add at least 50 per cent to your drive. I organised instant payment of the requisite number of shekels and waited patiently for it to arrive by post which it did with almost mystical speed. I strapped it to my bike and pedalled as fast as I could to the local golf range.

For starters the golf cover was enormous and I pulled it off to reveal a head bigger than the largest coconut you could win at a fair. The shaft was an inch or two longer as well, and the titanium 'skin' was gossamer thin. I ordered a basket of balls and headed off to the farthest bay to try it out, hoping that the fencing at the far end of the range would be high enough to contain my drive. I took a couple of practice swings then teed up my first ball. I swung easily.

Caramba! The noise was almost supersonic – whereas most modern metal woods have a noise like hitting the ball with a tin can, this was like smashing a cricket ball with a milk churn. The ball shot off like a rocket, going up and up, then quickly diving into the most vicious slice I have ever seen. It sailed over the side fence and went on and on. Everyone on the range looked my way, some clutching their ears in alarm, some cursing, others half ducking as if expecting a plane to hurtle through the wall. Then there was jack-knifing, belly laughter.

I exited fast round the end wall, leaving my basket of balls. The world's largest driver languishes gathering dust in a bag that contains only those so-called wonder clubs that I am too embarrassed to take out on the course.

Perhaps it is a little cruel to have put it out to pasture after only ever allowing it a single shot, but heck, I have some pride you know.

5

THE COURSES

'Golf is a day spent in a round of strenuous idleness.'
William Wordsworth (1770–1850),
Poet Laureate

In the beginning it is probable that golf was a relatively free and easy game, played across country towards targets that were agreed upon willy-nilly. Then it is likely that the odd landowner or two cut up rough and declared his land out of bounds to the disreputable bunch of lunatic 'gowffers' who were forever hacking their way over his precious acres. Their only recourse would be to establish a regular playing circuit, a course, where they could hack away to their hearts' content.

Except on a Sunday, of course! Oh yes, and during archery practice times as well. It is probable, therefore, that most of the original golf courses were established in remote areas and kept hidden from the law – the first golfers were probably like poachers, considered undesirable denizens of the greens and links.

This creates considerable difficulty for today's golf archaeologist, since there are likely to be few artefacts left of these ancient clandestine courses – the odd hole in the ground perhaps, or maybe the occasional overgrown bunker. Perhaps one day some Indiana Jones type will come up trumps and find the very first golf course. The trouble will of course be in proving that it was a golf course. Until that day, we will have to content ourselves with knowing where some of the first recorded golf was played.

THE OLDEST KNOWN COURSES

The North Inch at Perth

The very first reference that we have to golf being played is the year 1502, when King James IV, that well-known dentist and scholar, played at the North Inch at Perth. The word inch is thought to come from the Gaelic meaning 'water meadow', and the original course had 6 holes.

Happily, there is still a course on the North Inch, although it has undoubtedly been re-laid again since King James's day. It is an open parkland course played alongside the River Tay and I actually know it well, having played many times when I was a house surgeon at Perth Royal Infirmary.

Carnoustie

Not long after King James IV struck a ball in anger at Perth, one of his officers of the law, Sir Robert Maule of Panmure

(1493–1560), the sheriff of the county of Angus, played golf at the Barry links in 1527.

Carnoustie is famous the world over for its golf and has the Championship, Burnside and Buddon courses. The Championship has been dubbed 'Carnasty' on account of its difficulty.

When I was at university in Dundee I used to play on the Burnside course with my uncle, who fortuitously lived in Carnoustie, only really venturing onto the Championship when I hooked a drive over the Barry Burn onto it.

Like the North Inch at Perth, the original course no longer exists and the golf courses at Carnoustie cannot claim to be the oldest.

Royal Montrose

It is said that golf was played over Montrose Links in the county of Angus as long ago as 1562 and it is reputed to be the fifth oldest course in the world. Certainly it is the ninth oldest golf club, having been formed in 1810 as the Montrose Golf Club.

In 1845 Prince Albert bestowed his royal patronage on the club and it became the Royal Albert Golf Club. In 1986 it amalgamated with the Victoria Golf Club to become the Royal Montrose Golf Club. Its current patron is HRH Prince Andrew, Duke of York.

Musselburgh

The Old Links at Musselburgh is a delightful little course which actually can claim to be the oldest golf course in the world, as indicated by its entry as such in the *Guinness World Records*; what's more, it actually retains its original layout.

Mary, Queen of Scots played there in 1567 which we know because her half-brother, James Stewart, the Earl of Moray accused her of playing golf just a few days after the murder of her husband, Lord Darnley. To play

The honesty box – a common feature on Scottish golf courses

golf under such circumstances was considered unseemly but, strangely, no-one batted an eyelid when, some years before, King Henry VIII took time out to play tennis at Hampton Court while his wife Anne Boleyn was being beheaded at the Tower of London. The old Musselburgh course had 7 holes, but it was extended to 8 in 1832 and then to 9 in 1870.

This is a gem of a course that is actually contained within a horse racing track. You can hire hickory golf clubs and play the game as it was meant to be played.

St Andrews

The Old Course at St Andrews is considered to be the home of golf. That does not mean that it is the oldest course, but it just might be!

In 1552 it is recorded that the town elders decreed that the public were permitted to 'play at golf, football, schuting, at all gamis with all uther, as ever they pleis and in ony time.' It is highly likely that golf had been played there before then. How many holes it had to begin with is not known, but by 1764 it had 12 and of these, 10 had to be played twice, so the course was actually 22 holes. In that year the 'captain and gentlemen golfers' of the Society of St Andrews Golfers decided to shorten it by turning the short first 4 holes, which happened to be the last 4 as well, into 2 long holes. Thus, very significantly it became an 18-hole course and the blueprint of eighteen holes was established.

In 1834 King William IV became the Society of St Andrews Golfers' patron and the name was changed accordingly to the Royal & Ancient Golf Club of St Andrews. In 1897 the R&A, as it is known throughout the world, took over the rules of golf and codified them, so that it became the ruling authority for the rules all over the world, except for the USA and Mexico.

Sometime in the mid-nineteenth century the large double-greens that characterise St Andrews Old Course were established. It is now an entrancing golf course played back and forth along the coast with seven huge double greens, giving the player the real sense of going out and coming home. The vagaries of the winds and the tides mean that you could play the course fifty times and never have the same experience twice.

In 1854 the R&A clubhouse was built and in 1863 Old Tom Morris was appointed as the head greenkeeper. With his long grey bushy beard, he is not an obvious golfing hero, yet he went on to win the Open Championship on four occasions. More than that he separated the first and the seventeenth greens and reversed the direction of play so that it is now played anti-clockwise.

Leith Links

The Leith Links is another ancient course. It originally had 5 holes, all of them over 400 yards, so they would have been mighty long holes in the days of the wooden clubs. As we read about earlier, King James II banned golf on these links back in 1457, so it had clearly been a place to strike golf balls for quite some time.

Not content with all that history, Leith has another distinction. King Charles I was playing there in 1641 when he heard news about the Irish Rebellion – it apparently put him off his game and he foozled a couple of drives.

Most significantly, however, the Leith Links was the home of the Honourable Company of Edinburgh Golfers. They formed the first recognisable golf club and in 1744 they played the first club competition when they played for a silver club. It was won by John Rattray, the club's first captain.

DID YOU KNOW?

The tin cups of the world measure exactly 4¼ inches in diameter. The reason is that this was the size of the hole cutting instrument used at Musselburgh. In 1893 the Royal & Ancient Golf Club of St Andrews accepted that this was an ideal dimension for a golf hole and decreed that ever after it should be that size. Just imagine all those narrowly missed putts that you might have made if the chap who made that hole-cutter had made it a sensible 4½ inches.

FOLLOW THE FLAGS

With the double green it could of course be confusing as to which hole to aim at, so in 1857 red and white flags were introduced – white on the front nine and red on the back – at St Andrews. Thus 'outward' and 'inward' flags were introduced. Another standard was introduced to the game.

A FEW FACTS ABOUT THE OLD COURSE, ST ANDREWS

The Old Course is affectionately known throughout the world as The Old Lady of St Andrews

There are 112 bunkers

Hell Bunker on the long 14th is rightly named

The 17th is known as the Road Hole, because the road – which you play off if you land on it – runs alongside the green

The Road Hole Bunker on the 17th has dashed the hopes and the spirits of many golfers, including that of the Japanese golfer Tommy Nakajima (see the chapter on the majors)

TEEING GROUNDS

Up until the mid-nineteenth century there was no regulation teeing-off area separate from the hole. Indeed, because the greens as such did not exist, but were simply closely scythed areas, their care was not regarded as being of crucial importance. The original idea was that golf should be a continuous game, so one finished a hole then teed off within one club length of the hole! Old Tom Morris, being the sensible greenkeeper that he was, decided that this was foolish and introduced separate teeing areas. Ever since then the greenkeepers of the world have taken pride in manicuring their greens.

THE PACE OF THE GREENS – THE STIMPMETER

Virtually every golfer will at some time or another moan and groan at the pace of the greens. Too fast, too slow, too erratic. The poor old greenkeeper takes the flak, of course. Yet what a hard task it is to get all 18 greens playing at the same pace.

In 1935 while watching the US Open at Oakmont, the Massachusetts amateur champion, Edward Stimpson Snr watched Gene Sarazen putt a ball off the green and concluded that the green had been unfairly fast. He set himself the task of finding a way of making things fairer, by being able to measure the pace of the greens and thus came up with the idea of the Stimpmeter. Essentially it is an angled device that allows a ball to roll down a slide at a set velocity so that the distance in feet that it rolls on the green can be measured. In 1976 the USGA used it during the US Open at Atlanta and it then became an integral part of championship golf.

The greens are categorised into slow, medium and fast. A slow green rolls 4.5ft, a medium green 6.5ft and a fast green 8.5ft. For championships they are usually prepared much faster, as is witnessed in the greens at the Masters every year.

AND SOME OTHER GREAT COURSES

Muirfield

This is a private golf course overlooking the Firth of Forth and is home to the Honourable Company of Edinburgh Golfers as well as one of the Open Championship courses. As we read earlier the Company of Edinburgh Golfers is the oldest golf club in the world. The Muirfield course was actually built in 1891 and was designed by Old Tom Morris.

Pebble Beach Golf Links

This superb test of championship golf is to be found on the Monterey Peninsula in California, USA. It is a public course and is one of the courses that have hosted the US Open and the PGA. It was not designed by a professional golf architect, but by Jack

Neville, an amateur, and opened in 1919. A fine job he made of it, although he modestly asserted that nature made the course, 'all I did was find the holes.'

It has several really tough holes and no actual signature hole. The 7th is a short 100 yarder, but it looks impossible in bad weather, played from an elevated tee to a small hole surrounded by rocks and crashing waves. The 8th is a par 4 played with the ocean along the entire right of the hole. The drive has to be well struck onto a smallish landing area atop a cliff, from whence there is a tough approach shot down to another tricky green. Finally, the 17th is one of the most famous holes in the world with a long par 3 of around 200 yards played to a long sloping green. None of them are for the faint-hearted.

Prestwick

This course in Ayrshire is important as the site of the first great championship for the Championship Belt in 1860, which was won by Willie Park Snr from Musselburgh. He beat Old Tom Morris, the Prestwick greenkeeper, by two shots. To date it has hosted 11 Open Championships.

Royal Blackheath

In 1608 a 7-hole course was laid out at Blackheath, apparently by courtiers of King James I (VI of Scotland), since they were suffering from golfing withdrawals. It was the first golf course in England and Royal Blackheath Golf Club therefore has the distinction of being the oldest golf club in England.

Royal Liverpool

Founded in 1869 and laid out on the racecourse of the Liverpool Hunt Club by Robert Chambers and George Morris (the younger brother of Old Tom Morris), this course is usually referred to as Hoylake. It is the second oldest links in England and has been home to many great tournaments, including the British Amateur and the Open. The two great amateurs Harold Hilton and John Ball played at Hoylake and both won the Open as amateurs. It was also one of the courses upon which Bobby Jones won part of his grand slam in 1930.

Royal Calcutta

In 1829 the Dum Dum Golfing Club was formed at Calcutta in India. It later became the Royal Calcutta Golf Club, and it is the oldest golf club in the world outside the British Isles. It was followed in 1842 by the Bombay Golfing Society, which later became the Royal Bombay.

Royal Adelaide

In 1871 the Adelaide Golf Club was formed, but for some reason it only lasted a few years. It was resurrected on a different site in 1892 and in 1923 it became the Royal Adelaide. It is ranked in the top 100 courses in the world.

Royal Montreal

In 1873 a group of eight men, said to be officers of trading ships from Scotland, met in a dockside office and decided to form a golf club. They duly built a course and in 1884 were granted the right to call it the Royal Montreal Golf Club – it was the first permanent golf club on the American continent.

Royal Cape

In 1885 the first club was formed in Africa and it was built by Sir Henry D'Oyley Torrens. It has hosted the South Africa Open Championship on ten occasions.

Royal Malta

In 1888 Sir Henry D'Oyley Torrens founded the Royal Malta after he had been sent to his final posting as Governor and Commander-in-Chief at Malta.

Royal Troon

This great links course was founded in 1878 with just 5 holes. It is now (the Old Course) one of the courses used for the Open Championship and is distinguished by having both the longest and shortest holes in the competition. The longest is a huge 601 yards (or 550 metres) long and the shortest is a mere 123 yards, or 112 metres. The short length of this hole is made up by the diminutive green. Willie Park said that it was 'a pitching surface skimmed down to the size of a "Postage Stamp".' It is the name by which it is famous around the world.

There is a second course at Troon, called the Portland, which was another of the courses designed by Dr Alister MacKenzie.

Sawgrass

Officially, this course is the Tournament Players Club at Sawgrass, generally known as TPC at Sawgrass. It is at Ponte Vedra Beach in Florida and was built and opened in 1980 by Pete and Alice Dye, a renowned architect couple. Alice Dye was herself an amateur champion, so she brought a player's insight into golf design. The course is the home to the Players Championship, one of the championships often talked about as a fifth major.

The signature hole is the 17th, known as the Island Green. The hole is a mere 132 yards to an undulating green fronted by a small bunker, which apart from a thin path leading to it is virtually surrounded by water.

In the 1998 Players Championship Steve Lowery hit a wedge to the Island Green, only to see a seagull swoop and attempt to pick it up. After a few attempts it managed and flew off, but dropped it into the water. Fortunately, he gained relief under Rule 18 – since the bird was considered an outside agency, and he was permitted to replace the ball where it had originally landed on the green.

St Andrews, Yonkers

The name of John Reid is forever associated with the start of golf in the USA. Reid was a resident of Yonkers in New York, but was of Scottish descent. In his youth he had seen golf being played in Scotland and when a relative informed him that he was travelling to St Andrews Reid asked him to bring back clubs and balls. His relative did so and on 22 February 1888 he and some friends played an historic game of golf in the USA at Yonkers on a three-hole course of their design. In 1892 they extended the course to six holes. It was so successful and popular that in 1896 they bought a 60-acre site and laid out an eighteen-hole course. This course is regarded as the home of golf in the USA.

Sunningdale

There are two courses at Sunningdale Golf Club in the Berkshire countryside. The Old Course was designed by Willie Park Jnr, which was opened in 1901 and the New Course was designed by Harry Colt. It was one of the first successful inland golf clubs in the UK.

Bobby Jones considered it a superb course and actually used some of its features in the design of Augusta National. Over the years it has hosted many great tournaments, including the British Masters, the European Open, the Women's British Open and the Seniors British Open. It is also home to the Sunningdale Foursomes, a unique event which is open to amateurs and professionals, men and women. It is played under special handicap arrangements.

Wentworth

This course was established in 1925 at Virginia Water in Surrey, not far from Windsor Castle, and the clubhouse once belonged to the Duke of Wellington's brother-in-law. A developer, W.G. Tarrant had obtained land and planned to build luxury houses around a golf course. Harry Colt designed the course around the clubhouse which is where the PGA European Tour headquarters are nowadays based.

There are three full courses and a 9-hole par 3 course. The West Course is a magnificent test of golf, which is regularly used for events such as the BMW PGA, the Ryder Cup and the HSBC World Matchplay tournaments.

Winged Foot

This great course at Mamaroneck, New York, was the home club of the great Tommy Armour. It was built in 1921 by Albert Tillinghast, one of the eminent early golf architects and has hosted several US Opens, PGA and Amateur championships. It has also hosted two Women's Open championships.

HOWDAH YOU DRIVE OFF AN ELEPHANT?

In 1937 the Australian professional golfer Joe Kirkwood, the
1920 Australian Open and the 1933 Canadian Open champion,
did just that – he drove a ball from on top of a howdah on the
back of an elephant at the Royal Calcutta Gof Club.

GENE SARAZEN'S ACE IN THE HOLE

At the 1973 Open Gene Sarazen holed in one at the Postage
Stamp at the age of 71 years.

6

THE CHAMPIONSHIPS

The meeting of these champions proud,
Seemed like the bursting thunder-cloud.
Sir Walter Scott (1771–1832),
'The Lay of the Last Minstrel'

It is likely that golf was originally regarded as a game to be played by gentlemen, or at least by people who had sufficient funds to buy the prohibitively expensive clubs and balls. Golf clubs started to spring up all over the place and inevitably each club would have tournaments to find out who was their champion golfer.

THE AMATEUR CHAMPIONSHIPS

In 1857 the first of the proper golf championships began at Prestwick when the seven leading golf clubs of the day were sent a letter challenging them to send their top two players to compete. As it turned out, eleven clubs sent a pair of golfers and the first Amateur Championship match took place at St Andrews. A trophy was awarded to the winning pair who represented Royal Blackheath – George Glennie and Lieutenant J.C. Stewart.

The second championship was played in 1858, and the format was changed to a singles competition, which has been the way ever since, the winner being the publisher Robert Chambers.

A year later, in 1859, the first official Amateur Championship was played, when it was won by George Condie of Perth. The tournament had started and it has been competed for annually, apart from the war years by amateur golfers; nowadays it is played for by the best amateurs throughout the world.

In 1894 there were two amateur championships played in the USA and the following year the US Golf Association was formed, which organised the first US Amateur Championship and also the first US Open Championship.

THE OPEN

In 1859 Allan Robertson died. He was one of the greatest of the early golf professionals who seemed to have well nigh defeated all comers. Tragically, he never entered the history books as the winner of a major championship since they had not been introduced during his lifetime.

The face of golf, however, was soon to change as in 1860 the Prestwick Club held a championship for only professional golfers, who played for a championship belt – Willie Park Snr was the first winner.

The following year the first Open Championship was played at Prestwick which was open to both amateurs and professionals. The winner was none other than Old Tom Morris, so he is regarded as the first Open Champion, despite Willie Park Snr's win of the previous year, since amateurs had not been included in the field of players. Old Tom Morris won £6 along with the championship belt.

Some years later, his son, Young Tom Morris won three times in a row and was allowed to keep the belt in 1870. A claret jug made by Mackay, Cunningham & Co. of Edinburgh was introduced as the trophy in 1873 and it became one of the most coveted trophies in sport. Its correct name is the Golf Championship Trophy although everyone knows it as the Claret Jug.

The Open is the oldest of the four major championships and is the only one to be played outside the USA. The first ten championships were administered by Prestwick Club, but then the baton was handed to the Royal & Ancient who have run it ever since. There were no tournaments in the years 1915 to 1919, nor 1940 to 1945, because of the First and Second World Wars.

The Open is only played on one of nine links courses in England or Scotland over 72 holes, a cut in the field being made after 36 holes.

DID YOU KNOW?

The Open has only been won by amateurs on six occasions:

Bobby Jones – 1926, 1927, 1930

Harold Hilton – 1892, 1897

John Ball – 1890

MULTIPLE OPEN CHAMPIONSHIP WINNERS

Golf champions who won the Claret Jug four or more times:

Harry Vardon – 6 wins – 1896, 1898, 1899, 1903, 1911, 1914

James Braid – 5 wins – 1901, 1905, 1906, 1908, 1910

Peter Thomson – 5 wins – 1954, 1955, 1956, 1958, 1965

Tom Watson – 5 wins – 1975, 1977, 1980, 1982, 1983

Old Tom Morris – 4 wins – 1861, 1862, 1864, 1867

Young Tom Morris – 4 wins – 1868, 1869, 1870, 1872

(no championship played in 1871)

Willie Park Snr – 4 wins – 1860, 1863, 1866, 1875 (although 1860 was a professional only championship)

J.H. Taylor – 4 wins – 1894, 1895, 1900, 1909

Walter Hagen – 4 wins – 1922, 1924, 1928, 1929

Modern great players who have won three Opens include Jack Nicklaus, Seve Ballesteros, Sir Nick Faldo, Tiger Woods, Gary Player, Henry Cotton, and the great Bobby Jones.

A DROP IN THE SAND

In the 1978 Open at St Andrews Tommy Nakajima took a 9 on the 17th hole to drop out of contention. He had been 4 under, but putted off the green on the 17th into the dreaded hole, needing 4 shots to get out.

THE INCREDIBLE GARY PLAYER

Gary Player is the only golfer to have won the Open in three different decades, winning the Claret Jug in 1959, 1968 and 1974.

THE US OPEN

This great tournament began in 1895 at the Newport Country Club in Rhode Island. It was a 9-hole course and the first championship was played over 36 holes in a single day. The Championship is run by the United States Golf Association, the USGA, and has been played every year except for 1917 and 1918 and between 1942 and 1945. It is nowadays played over four rounds, as are the other major championships. Unlike the others, however, if there is a tie after four rounds then a further 18 holes are played, only then going into sudden death. It is timed so that it ends on Father's Day.

GLORIOUS US OPEN AMATEUR CHAMPIONS

To win this event as an amateur golfer is a phenomenal achievement, which one doubts could be done in the modern era. Yet who knows, perhaps another titan of the game like Bobby Jones has yet to pick up his clubs for the first time with destiny beckoning. We live in hope.

Bobby Jones – 4 wins – 1923, 1926, 1929, 1930

Francis Ouimet – 1 win – 1913

Jerome Travers – 1 win – 1915

Chick Evans – 1 win – 1916

Johnnie Goodman – 1 win – 1933

MULTIPLE US OPEN CHAMPIONS

Only four players have so far won the US Open Championship four times. Bobby Jones is the only amateur to have won it several times:

Willie Anderson – 4 wins – 1901, 1903, 1904, 1905

Bobby Jones – 4 wins – 1923, 1926, 1929, 1930

Ben Hogan – 4 wins – 1948, 1950, 1951, 1953

Jack Nicklaus – 4 wins – 1962, 1967, 1972, 1980

Modern great players who have won three times, to date, are Tiger Woods, Hale Irwin.

KNOCKED OUT AT THE US OPEN

In 1934 Bobby Cruickshank was leading the tournament, but after hitting a spectacular shot he threw his club in the air. It landed on his head and knocked him out. He recovered consciousness, but lost his rhythm and, consequently, the tournament.

THE MASTERS

This great tournament began in 1934 at the Augusta National Golf Club in Georgia. It is competed for every April on what must be one of the most beautiful and carefully manicured courses in the world. Magnolias abound, the caddies all wear uniform white overalls, white tennis shoes and green caps, and the actual greens are as fast as ice.

The course was founded by the great Bobby Jones and Clifford Roberts, a New York banker, and designed by Alister MacKenzie on the site of an old Indigo plantation.

The field in The Masters is the smallest of any of the majors, since the tournament is, and always has been, an invitational.

The trophy for this event is a coveted Green Jacket, which the champion keeps for a year. They then have to hand it back to the club. The champion from the previous year traditionally helps him on with it. They also receive a gold medal and have their name engraved on a silver trophy, which is modelled on the clubhouse. They get to keep a facsimile.

DR ALISTER MacKENZIE – THE CAMOUFLAGE SURGEON

The designer of the great Augusta National Golf Club, Dr Alister MacKenzie (1870–1934) was born in Normanton in Yorkshire and trained as a surgeon. He served as a doctor during the Boer War and again during the First World War. Fascinatingly, it wasn't his surgical skills that were used in the First World War, but his ability as a camoufleur. During the Boer War he had studied the way that the Boers had used camouflage to maximum effect and this he used in the war effort – and again when he turned to golf course design after the war.

He wrote a book, *Golf Architecture*, in which he said, 'The chief object of every golf course architect worth his salt is to imitate the beauties of nature so closely as to make his work indistinguishable from nature itself.'

As well as the Augusta National, he built many great courses around the world, including Cypress Point Club, the Royal Melbourne Club and Moortown and Alwoodley, two courses in Leeds, not far from his place of birth.

Augusta National was opened and ready to play in 1933, but sadly, he died in 1934 the year that the course hosted its first Invitational Tournament.

MULTIPLE MASTERS CHAMPIONS

No amateur has ever won the Masters. Here are some of the professionals who have won it the most.:

Jack Nicklaus has won 6 Green Jackets – 1963, 1965, 1966, 1972, 1975, 1986

Arnold Palmer has won 4 Green Jackets – 1958, 1960, 1962, 1964

Tiger Woods has won 4 Green Jackets – 1997, 2001, 2002, 2005

Gary Player has won 3 Green Jackets – 1961, 1974, 1978

Sam Snead won 3 Green Jackets – 1949, 1952, 1954,

Sir Nick Faldo has won 3 Green Jackets – 1989, 1990, 1996

Phil Mickelson has won 3 Green Jackets – 2004, 2006, 2010

Jimmy Demaret has won 3 Green Jackets – 1940, 1947, 1950

Several great golfers have won twice, including – Byron Nelson, Horton Smith, Ben Hogan, Tom Watson, Seve Ballesteros, Bernhard Langer and José María Olazábal.

THE HAZARD OF RAE'S CREEK

Rae's Creek snakes its way across the south-eastern part of the Augusta National, coming into play on the 11th, 12th and 13th holes. Poor Tommy Nakajima had a rough time in 1978 during both the Open and the Masters. In the 1978 Masters he incurred five penalty shots after knocking his ball in Rae's Creek while playing the 13th. He grounded his club in the hazard, the ball hit his foot and he ended up taking a 13.

A SCORING MISTAKE

In the 1968 Masters Roberto de Vicenzo signed his card without noticing that his playing partner had mistakenly added an extra stroke to the score on one hole. He signed, so he had to accept the score, which meant he had one too many – and he lost the title.

THE US PGA CHAMPIONSHIP

The United States Professional Golfers' Association Championship, usually simply known as the PGA is generally regarded as the fourth major golf championship. It was established in 1916 and is usually played in mid-August. It is the last of the four majors every year. Rod Wanamaker, a wealthy financier donated the fabulous Wanamaker Trophy, which the field plays for. The winner is given a replica to keep for a year and a smaller version to keep for ever.

The tournament is played on a number of courses, but tends to be played in the eastern states.

No amateur has ever won the PGA, since it is for professional golfers only. It is the main major which will give the top club professionals an opportunity to play.

MULTIPLE PGA CHAMPIONS

Walter Hagen – 1921, 1924, 1925, 1926, 1927

Jack Nicklaus – 1963, 1971, 1973, 1975, 1980

Tiger Woods – 1999, 2000, 2006, 2007

Gene Sarazen – 1922, 1923, 1933

Sam Snead – 1942, 1949, 1951

There have been many two-time winners, including Ben Hogan, Gary Player, Dave Stockton, Ray Floyd, Lee Trevino, Larry Nelson, Nick Price and Vijay Singh.

CAREER GRAND SLAMS

There have been five players who have made career grand slams, having won each of the majors at least once.

Gene Sarazen

Ben Hogan

Gary Player

Jack Nicklaus

Tiger Woods

ANYONE IN THE FIELD CAN WIN

One would have expected that the leading players should be the ones who regularly win majors, however, in recent years it has become very difficult to predict who will win.

In 2010 there were three first-time major champions:

US Open – Graeme McDowell (Northern Ireland)
The Open – Louis Oosthuizen (South Africa)
PGA – Martin Kaymer – Germany

In 2011 there were four first-time major champions:

Masters – Charl Schwartzel (South Africa)
US Open – Rory McIlroy (Northern Ireland)
The Open – Darren Clarke (Northern Ireland)
PGA – Keegan Bradley (USA)

It could be said that winning a major has become a bit of a lottery. More correctly it should be said that the quality of play is so high that almost anyone can win.

BUT SOME GOLFERS ARE DESTINED TO BE CHAMPIONS

Rory McIlroy demonstrated a prodigious talent from an early age. The Northern Ireland golfer had a successful amateur career then proceeded to shine on the professional tour. He played in the 2010 Ryder Cup and seemed to have the 2011 Masters sewn up when he led for three days. His fourth round was disastrous and he shot an 80, which dropped him into a tie for 15th place. People wondered whether it would destroy him – it certainly did not. He bounced back at the 2011 US Open at Congressional and won by 8 shots. He is undoubtedly destined for many more successes.

THE WOMEN'S MAJOR CHAMPIONSHIPS

Women's professional golf has two main tours. The oldest is the LPGA, the Ladies Professional Golf Association, which was founded in 1950 and is based in Daytona Beach, Florida, in the USA. The younger is the LET, Ladies European Tour, which was founded in 1979 by the Women's Professional Golf Association, WPGA.

The LPGA is a huge tour with huge prize money while the LET is gradually catching up and currently runs about 28 events in 19 countries around the world, with players from 38 countries.

The Majors
There are currently four major events recognised by the LPGA. These are:

Kraft Nabisco Championship

LPGA Championship

U.S. Women's Open

Women's British Open

The LET runs the Women's British Open, but it is the only one of the four that is played in Britain, the others are all played in the USA.

The number of majors has varied over the years and no-one has won a four-major grand slam although the American Babe Zaharias won all three available majors in 1950. Six women golfers have won career grand slams, in that they have won four major titles not in the same years. They are:

Pat Bradley

Juli Inkster

Annika Sörenstam

Louise Suggs

Karrie Webb

Mickey Wright

Karrie Webb has in fact won a super career grand slam, since she has won five of the majors, having triumphed in the du Maurier Classic in 1999 when it was one of the majors.

7

THE GOLFING GREATS

'Some men give up their designs when they have almost reached the goal; While others, on the contrary, obtain a victory by exerting, at the last moment, more vigorous efforts than ever before.'
Herodotus (*c.* 484–25 BC),
Ancient Greek historian

The game of golf is so difficult that ordinary amateurs can merely wonder at the skills possessed by those golfers who went out there and repeatedly produced great scores in the crucible of intense competition. What follows is a list of some of those great golfers each with a vignette to give a flavour of their prowess.

ALLAN ROBERTSON (1815–59)

This great golfer was one of the first professionals. Born in St Andrews, he is said to have never been beaten when playing for money and was greatly revered by his fellow players. It is sad that he is not recorded in the annals of golf as a champion, since he played and lived before the establishment of the Open.

Robertson was a third generation ball- and club-maker and exported his wares all over the world, as golf was becoming established by travellers taking the game abroad. His young apprentice would become known as Old Tom Morris, and would achieve the golfing immortality that was denied to Allan. They often partnered each other, and predictably, were well nigh unbeatable.

Unfortunately, it was the introduction of the gutty that broke their relationship. Allan caught Tom playing with the new gutty instead of the featherie ball and sacked him on the spot. He clearly viewed the gutty as an abhorrence.

OLD TOM MORRIS (1821–1908)

Thomas Mitchell Morris Snr, known to history as Old Tom Morris to distinguish him from his son Young Tom Morris, was born in St Andrews. There is a delightful tale about him starting to play golf at the age of ten, by knocking improvised balls made from wine corks, weighted down with nails about the streets of the old town. Like other young lads in the town he started caddying and at the age of fourteen was taken on as an apprentice with Allan Robertson. He learned from him all the skills of golf and the techniques of ball- and club-making. In 1851, he was sacked after Allan Robertson caught him playing with a gutty ball. He then obtained a position at Prestwick and designed the Old Course there. He ran a successful business and was instrumental in establishing the Open, which was played there in 1860, the year after Allan Robertson died. Old Tom drove the first ball in the championship, which that year was won by Willie Park Snr, with Old Tom coming second.

Old Tom Morris and his son,
Young Tom Morris

In 1864 he returned to St Andrews as professional golfer and greenkeeper and set about establishing the Old Course. He then had a successful career designing courses around Britain, including Prestwick, Carnoustie, Muirfield, Askernish on South Uist and Westward Ho! in Devon.

He won the Open in 1861, 1862, 1864 and 1867 and was inducted into the World Golf Hall of Fame in 1976.

WILLIE PARK SNR (1833–1903)

William Park was born in Musselburgh and learned to play on its links as well as at St Andrews. He was one of the early greats and was a contemporary of Old Tom Morris. He started his working life as a caddie then became a professional golfer and a club-maker. He won four Open Championships, including the first one and his brother Mungo Park also won it once.

He was inducted into the World Golf Hall of Fame in 2005.

YOUNG TOM MORRIS (1851–75)

Born and bred in St Andrews, Young Tom Morris learned all he knew from his father, Old Tom Morris. In his early days Old Tom was the professional at Prestwick, which is where Young Tom learned the game. Then his father moved back to St Andrews as the professional and greenkeeper and Young Tom completed his golf education on the Old Course.

He won four straight Open Championships in 1868, 1869, 1870 and 1872 (there had been no championship in 1871) and all were played at Prestwick, a course that he literally knew like the back of his hand. His first win was at the remarkably early age of 17. He was permitted to keep the championship belt after his hat trick of wins and when the Claret Jug was established as the prize, his name was the first to be engraved upon it after his win in 1872.

Sadly, he died on Christmas Day 1875 at the age of twenty-four. He and his father had been playing Willie Park Snr and his brother Mungo Park at Prestwick (and winning) when Young Tom received a telegram to say that he was needed at home, where his wife had gone into a difficult labour. They finished the match, which they won, then hurried back to St Andrews. Tragically, both his wife and child were dead and a mere 4 months later, Young Tom Morris, perhaps the greatest played that ever wielded a golf club, was also dead.

He was inducted into the World Golf Hall of Fame in 1975.

WILLIE PARK JNR (1864–1925)

The son of the great champion, Willie Park Snr, like his father Willie Park Jnr ran a golf equipment business and was an excellent player, winning the Open twice and being in the top ten twelve times. He wrote two major books, *The Game of Golf* in 1896 and *The Art of Putting* in 1920. He also invented and patented numerous clubs. As a golf course architect he designed over 170 courses around the world, including the Old Course at Sunningdale, the Weston Golf Club in Toronto and Olympia Fields in Chicago.

THE WORLD GOLF HALL OF FAME

To become a member of the World Golf Hall of Fame is one of the great accolades in golf. The World Golf Hall of Fame is situated in St Augustine in Florida, having originally been based in Pinehurst, North Carolina. It is supported by 26 golf organisations from around the world and was established in 1974, when the names of thirteen golfers were inducted. There are five categories – PGA Tour/Champions Tour, LPGA, International, Lifetime achievement and Veterans. New inductees are elected every year.

THE FIRST MAJOR HOLE IN ONE

Young Tom Morris holed the 166-yard 8th at Prestwick in the Open Championship of 1868.

THREE GREAT AMATEURS

John Ball (1861–1940)

John Ball Jnr was an amateur golfer from Liverpool who won 8 British Amateur Championships and the Open in 1890.

He was inducted into the World Golf Hall of Fame in 1977.

Harold Horsfall Hilton (1869–1942)

Harold Hilton was an amateur golfer from West Kirby who won the Open Championship twice, in 1892 and 1897. In addition, he won the British Amateur championship four times and the US Amateur championship once.

He was inducted into the World Golf Hall of Fame in 1978.

Johnny Laidlay (1860–1940)

John Ernest Laidlay was another great amateur golfer who reached the heights in the Victorian era. He was born near to North Berwick and learned his golf there and at Musselburgh. He won over 130 amateur titles, including the British Amateur in 1889 and 1891. In 1893 he was runner-up in the Open to Willie Auchterlonie.

He was a renowned putter, albeit he used a highly unorthodox looking style, which you can see in the chapter on putting. Yet perhaps his greatest service to golf was in inventing the overlapping golf grip that is nowadays used by the vast majority of gofers around the world. He was never given the credit for it, unfortunately, since Harry Vardon used it and it has become known as the Vardon grip ever since.

The overlapping grip invented by Johnny Laidlay and adopted by Harry Vardon. It is now universally known as the Vardon Grip.

FRANCIS OUIMET (1893–1967)

Francis Ouimet was born in Brookline, Massachusetts, USA. His father was a French-Canadian immigrant and his mother was an Irish immigrant and the family lived opposite the 17th hole of the Country Club in Brookline. Francis was entirely self-taught and his skills came to the attention of the caddie master and some of the club members. He won several regional amateur tournaments and was asked by the US Golf Association to compete at the Country Club at Brookline in the US Open of 1913 which he did and duly tied for the lead with Harry Vardon and Ted Ray, beating them in the play-off. He was the first American to be elected captain of the Royal & Ancient Golf Club of St Andrews. He was inducted into the World Golf Hall of Fame in 1974.

THE GREAT TRIUMVIRATE

Golf is a classic game and it is interesting that a classical term is used to describe three of the greatest golfers of the late nineteenth and early twentieth century. A triumvirate refers to a system in which three shared power. It is perhaps justified when used to refer to these three as between them they notched up sixteen Open titles.

Harry Vardon (1870–1937)

Born in Jersey into a family of modest means, Harry Vardon rose to become the pre-eminent golfer of his age. He moved to England and became a professional golfer, winning a record six Opens and one US Open. The latter was achieved in 1900 when he went on an exhibition tour of the USA in order to promote his own gutty, the Vardon Flyer.

He is credited with having invented the Vardon grip, the overlapping grip that is used nowadays by the majority of golfers, although he had followed Johnny Laidlay, who actually was the first to use it. He was also the first professional golfer to be known for sartorial elegance when he started to wear plus twos, instead of straight long trousers or plus fours.

He was inducted into the World Golf Hall of Fame in 1974.

The Great Triumvirate – J.H. Taylor, James Braid and Harry Vardon.

James Braid (1870–1950)

James Braid was born at Earlsferry in the Kingdom of Fife. He went on to win five Opens, but never competed in America.

As a golf course architect he designed both the King's Course and the Queen's Course at Gleneagles. He is also attributed as the inventor of the dogleg, an accolade he shares with J.H. Taylor, his fellow member of the Great Triumvirate.

He was inducted into the World Golf Hall of Fame in 1976.

J.H. Taylor (1871–1963)

John Henry Taylor, commonly referred to as J.H. Taylor, was born in Devon. At the age of 11 he started caddying at Westward Ho in Devon and became a professional at the age of 19.

He won five Open Championships and was runner-up in the 1900 US Open behind Harry Vardon.

He was also a co-founder of the PGA and its first chairman and, like his colleague James Braid, he designed golf courses and was said to be the originator of the dogleg.

I actually used to play at Batchwood Hall in St Albans, which was built according to his design in 1935 and know all five of his doglegs pretty well. I used to wish, however, that he had given the course an anatomically normal four dog legs.

Taylor was inducted into the World Golf Hall of Fame in 1975.

BUT IT SHOULD HAVE BEEN A GREAT QUADRUMVIRATE!

Ted Ray (1877–1943)

Edward R.G. Ray, known as Ted Ray, was perhaps a little unfortunate to have been playing during the reign of the Great Triumvirate yet it is rather unkind of posterity to have excluded him, since he won the Open in 1912 and the US Open in 1920. He was born and bred in Jersey, like Harry Vardon. He was a big man and hit a long ball and usually he is shown playing golf with a pipe clenched betwixt his teeth. That can't be easy, but looking nonchalant never is, especially on a golf course.

In 1913 he played in the US Open with Harry Vardon and Francis Ouimet, who was an amateur. They tied for the lead, but against the odds Ouimet won the play-off. The story is depicted in the 2005 film *The Greatest Game Ever Played*, which was based on the book of the same name by Mark Frost.

THE GREATEST AMATEUR GOLFER OF ALL TIME

Bobby Jones (1902–71)

Robert Tyre Jones Jnr was a remarkable man. He held several degrees and was a lawyer by profession, who happened to play competitive golf. Indeed, he was the most successful amateur golfer of all time and arguably may have been the greatest golfer of all time.

He won just about everything he entered including four US Opens, three Opens, five US Amateurs and one British

Amateur. These tournaments were all regarded as majors at the time, and Bobby Jones referred to them as the 'Impregnable Quadrilateral'. Effectively, he suggested that no-one could win all four. However, in 1930 he placed a bet on himself that he could achieve that, which he duly did. Hence the concept of the grand slam was conceived.

Bobby Jones retired from competitive golf at the age of 28 and was instrumental in building Augusta National and in establishing the Masters, which has been played there regularly ever since, apart from the years of the Second World War. He was inducted into the World Golf Hall of Fame in 1974. Don't confuse him with Robert Trent Jones (1906–2000), who was a golf course architect, who designed some 500 courses around the world.

Bobby Jones.

WALTER HAGEN (1892–1969)

Walter Hagen was a champagne golfer – that is, he adopted a high society lifestyle and played effervescent golf. He was instrumental in starting international team matches and starting and maintaining the Ryder Cup.

Tournament professionals today have much to thank him for, since he almost single-handedly elevated the status of the professional golfer. The story goes that at the 1932 Open at Sandwich he was refused entry to the clubhouse, since professionals were not allowed in. He immediately rented a prestigious car and chauffeur and parked it the drive in front of the clubhouse, where he was served a champagne luncheon. He went on to win the Open, but refused to go into the clubhouse afterwards.

His clubs did a lot of the talking when he was quiet long enough to take a shot. He recognised that professionals were entertainers and he certainly entertained. He is the third most successful major winner of all time, behind Jack Nicklaus and Tiger Woods.

He won two US Opens, four Opens and five PGA championships (only the Masters evaded him).

He was inducted into the World Golf Hall of Fame in 1974.

GENE SARAZEN (1902–99)

Gene Sarazen was a regular guy but he had a career grand slam and won seven majors, including one Masters, one Open, two US Opens and three PGA championships.

In the 1935 Masters he hit 'the shot that was heard around the world' – a 235-yard 4-wood into the hole at the 15th for an albatross (a double eagle or three under par on a par 5). This allowed him to catch Craig Wood who was leading the tournament. He tied and then won the play-off the following day.

Gene Sarazen was given the rare honour of being made an honorary member of the Royal & Ancient Golf Club of St Andrews and he was inducted into the World Golf Hall of Fame in 1974.

THE INVENTOR OF THE SAND WEDGE

Appropriately enough, while playing at Sandwich in the 1932 Open, Gene Sarazen exposed his secret weapon. He had soldered lead onto the back of a thin-bladed niblick to produce a wedge-like club that could explode the ball from the bunker. He won the Open and the sand wedge was born.

SAM SNEAD (1912–2000)

Samuel Jackson Snead was one of the most charismatic golfers, a natural entertainer who cracked jokes, danced and realised which side his bread was buttered. He was a big hitter, hence his nickname of 'Slammin' Sammy'.

He accumulated seven major wins, including three Masters, three PGAs and one Open. He never quite clinched the US Open, but came runner-up on four occasions.

In his later career he developed the yips and began using a croquet mallet style whereby he straddled the line of the putt and struck the ball between his legs. Auric Goldfinger uses this style in Ian Fleming's novel, *Goldfinger*. The method was banned by the USGA and Snead thought his career was over, having cured his yips with the croquet style. Then he remembered seeing an old-timer in England putt in much the same way but without actually straddling the line. He then started using a side-saddle method which was legal.

He was inducted into the World Golf Hall of Fame in 1974.

BEN HOGAN (1912–97)

William Ben Hogan was the quiet man of golf and was sometimes called 'The Wee Iceman', because he concentrated so intensely on the course. He was an avid analyst of the game who made practice the norm in professional golf. He was a relatively late starter in accumulating his major tally, but with nine to his credit he showed what a gifted golfer he was.

His early life was marred by tragedy as his father committed suicide and the family were left in dire straits. Ben left college before his 18th birthday and turned professional. His first major victory did not come until he won the PGA at the age of thirty-four. From then on, he concentrated and won two Masters, four US Opens, one Open and two PGA championships – all this despite serving in the Second World War and also having to recover from a near-fatal car accident.

In his book *Ben Hogan's Five Lessons: the Modern Fundamentals of Golf*, which he wrote in 1957, he said that he believed any golfer of average coordination could, with intelligence and practice of the fundamentals of the swing, be able to break 80. His book has been of inestimable value to both professionals and amateurs ever since and he was inducted into the World Golf Hall of Fame in 1974.

TOMMY ARMOUR (1894–1968)

Thomas Dickson Armour was born and educated in Edinburgh, served in the Tank Corps during the First World War and was discharged at the rank of major. He had been exposed to mustard gas during an explosion and suffered visual loss as a result. He recovered vision in his right eye and only took up golf then, becoming, according to some, the finest iron player of his age.

After the First World War he moved to America and was taken under Walter Hagen's wing. He turned professional in 1924 and won the 1927 US Open, the 1930 PGA and the 1931 Open.

He was inducted into the World Golf Hall of Fame in 1976.

A RARE BIRD INDEED

At the 1927 Shawnee Open Tommy Armour inexplicably shot an 'archaeopteryx', when he had a 15 or more over par, in Armour's case 18 over par, hitting 23 on a par 5 hole.

SIR HENRY COTTON (1907–87)

Henry Cotton was the finest British golfer between the wars. He turned professional at the age of 17 and was renowned, rather like Ben Hogan, for the amount that he practiced.

He won three Open Championships, two before the Second World War and one after, in 1948.

He died on 27 December 1987 and was knighted in the 1988 New Year's Honours List. Sadly he had died before he was actually dubbed, but he had been aware that he had been given the great award for his contribution to golf.

He was inducted into the World Golf Hall of Fame in 1980.

A ROUND IMMORTALISED

Henry Cotton scored a 65 in the final round of the 1934 Open. In his honour the Dunlop Company began manufacturing Dunlop 65 balls.

BYRON NELSON (1912–2006)

John Byron Nelson Jnr was a Texan who turned professional at the age of 20. He is credited as being the father of the modern golf swing, because he introduced leg action into the downswing to generate extra power.

He won five majors, including two Masters, two PGAs and one US Open, and the Byron Nelson Classic tournament is named in his honour.

He was inducted into the World Golf Hall of Fame in 1974.

ARNOLD PALMER

Arnold Daniel Palmer was born in Latrobe, Pennsylvania, in 1929, the son of a golf professional and greenkeeper. He became known as the 'King', and has been one of the most charismatic and most popular golfers of the modern era. His followers were dubbed Arnie's Army.

Arnold Palmer has always played with an ungainly looking swing in which he launches his whole weight into the ball. Never one to take the safe option, he played with abandon, which made him so exciting to watch.

He won seven majors, including four Masters, two Opens and one US Open. He never managed the PGA, but was runner-up on three occasions.

In addition to those wins and numerous ones on both the PGA and Champions tours, he has won five Champions Tour majors. He is widely and rightly regarded as one of the finest ambassadors for golf. He was made an honorary member of the Royal & Ancient Golf Club of St Andrews and in 2010 he was awarded an honorary doctorate of Law by the University of St Andrews.

He was inducted into the World Golf Hall of Fame in 1974.

PETER THOMSON

Peter William Thomson was born in Brunswick in Australia in 1929. He won national titles in ten countries around the world and won the Open Championship five times. That includes an astonishing run of three successive victories, in 1954, 1955 and 1956. He then won again in 1958 and 1965.

He was inducted into the World Golf Hall of Fame in 1988.

GARY PLAYER

Gary Player is the most successful international golfer of all time. He was born in Johannesburg in 1935. He bubbles with energy, takes his fitness incredibly seriously and has been a success in many spheres of life. He practices and he competes to the utmost of his considerable ability. Over the years Player had gathered several nicknames, including the 'Black Knight' for his tendency to dress in black on the course, and the 'International Ambassador of Golf', because of his globe-trotting to play in tournaments. He has notched up a staggering air mileage.

Gary Player has accumulated nine majors on the regular tour and several others on the Champions Tour. These include a career grand slam and the unique record of having won the

Open in three different decades. He has also won three Masters, three Opens, two PGAs and one US Open.

Among his many accolades, he was awarded an honorary Doctorate of Law from St Andrews University in 1995 and was inducted into the World Golf Hall of Fame in 1974.

He now runs a successful golf course design business and a stud farm, but still plays and competes. He is also involved in charitable and philanthropic work.

A GREAT MODERN AMATEUR – SIR MICHAEL BONALLACK

This great English amateur golfer was born at Chigwell in Essex in 1934. He won many amateur honours, including five Amateur Championships and five English Amateur Championships. He was secretary of the Royal & Ancient from 1984 to 1990 and was also captain in 2000. He was inducted into the World Golf Hall of Fame in 2000.

SIR BOB CHARLES

Robert James Charles is the most successful New Zealand golfer of all times, who has won more than seventy times around the world. He was born in Carterton on New Zealand's North Island in 1937. He is the most famous left-handed golfer in the world and won the Open in 1963.

He was knighted in 1999 and awarded the Order of New Zealand in 2010. He was inducted into the World Golf Hall of Fame in 2008.

JACK NICKLAUS

Jack William Nicklaus was born in Columbus, Ohio, in 1940 and attended Ohio State University. He won two US Amateur championships and then turned professional at the age of 21. In 1962 he won the US Open, defeating the enormously popular Arnold Palmer, much to the chagrin of Arnie's Army. It was not long before Jack Nicklaus gathered his own following, for he played an equally exciting brand of golf. He could play all manner of shots and was also a great long hitter, becoming affectionately known as the 'Golden Bear'.

Jack Nicklaus won eighteen majors on the regular tour and went on to claim more on the seniors. He holds numerous records and many say that his record speaks for itself; he is the greatest player of all time. He won six Masters, the last at the age of 46; four US Opens, three Opens and five PGA championships.

Jack Nicklaus is a great sportsman and his name is synonymous with fair play. Like Gary Player, he was awarded an honorary Doctorate of Law by the University of St Andrews in 1984 and he is also an honorary member of the Royal & Ancient Golf Club of St Andrews.

He was inducted into the World Golf Hall of Fame in 1974 and is still heavily involved in golf course design and charity work.

TOM WATSON

Thomas Sturges Watson was born in Kansas City, Missouri, in 1949 and has a degree in psychology.

With his youthful good looks he soon became a favourite of the golfing world, and he has won eight majors and gone on to win several more on the Champions Tour. His majors include five Opens, two Masters and one US Open. He was beaten by Seve Ballesteros in the 1984 Open when he was vying to equal Harry Vardon's record of six Open victories. Then unfortunately, he just failed to win the 2009 Open at Turnberry when after leading after the second and third rounds and for most of the final round, he hit an approach shot too well and was unlucky for it to skip through the green into the rough at the fringe of the green. He bogeyed the hole and ended up in a play-off with Stewart Cink, who went on to win the 4-hole game. Stewart Cink deserved his win, but had Tom Watson won he would have been the oldest Open champion, being almost 60 years old.

In 2010 he was awarded an honorary Doctorate of Law by the University of St Andrews and he is also an honorary member of the Royal & Ancient Golf Club of St Andrews.

He was inducted into the World Golf Hall of Fame in 1988.

LEE TREVINO

Lee Trevino, known in the golfing world as either 'Super Mex' or 'Merry Mex', was born outside Dallas, Texas, in 1939. He had a hard beginning and started working in the cotton fields in Texas at the age of 5. His uncle gave him an old golf club and a few balls and he discovered an amazing talent; at 8 he started caddying and with diligent practice could perform amazing shots. He became a club professional in El Paso at the age of 21.

His laughter was infectious, his banter was witty and the crowds loved him as he won six majors, including two US Opens, two Opens and two PGAs.

He was inducted into the World Golf Hall of Fame in 1981.

TONY JACKLIN

Anthony Jacklin, known as Tony Jacklin, was born in Scunthorpe, North Lincolnshire, in 1944. He turned professional in 1962 and has won two majors and lifted the spirit of British and European golf when he won the Open in 1969 and the US Open in 1970 – it was the first time that a British golfer had won the US Open since Harry Vardon's victory in 1900. He was narrowly beaten in the 1971 Open by Lee Trevino.

As a Ryder Cup captain, he was truly inspirational and is the most successful captain of all time in the competition.

In 1990 he was awarded the CBE (Commander of the British Empire) and was inducted into the World Golf Hall of Fame in 2002.

RAY FLOYD

Raymond Loran Floyd was born in Fort Bragg, North Carolina, in 1942. He maintained a superb golf game throughout a long career, accumulating many wins worldwide, and was one of the oldest players to win both a major and a regular PGA tour event.

He won four majors, including two PGAs, one Masters and one US Open. He was a regular Ryder Cup player and captained the American team in 1989.

He was inducted into the World Golf Hall of Fame in 1989.

CURTIS STRANGE

Curtis Northrup Strange was born in Norfolk, Virginia, in 1955. He was the first professional golfer to make a million dollars in prize money in one season. He won back-to-back US Opens in 1988 and 1989 and was also the runner-up in one Masters and one PGA. He was a regular Ryder Cup player and captained the USA team in 2002.

He was inducted into the World Golf Hall of Fame in 2007.

SEVE BALLESTEROS (1957–2011)

Severiano Ballesteros was born in Pedreña in Spain in 1957. The youngest of five brothers, three of his siblings also became golf professionals, but Seve, as he was always known, was to become one of the most talented players ever to hold a golf club. He was virtually self-taught, having found out how to play all manner of shots with a cut-down 3 iron. This ability never left him, and while he could be wild from the tee – he was known as the car park golfer for a long time, because of errant tee shots – he could conjure up wondrous approaches from anywhere.

He won five majors, including three Opens and two Masters. As a team player he was phenomenal, both in singles and in paired play, and he was also a successful Ryder Cup captain.

He was the recipient of an honorary Doctorate of Law from the University of St Andrews and was inducted into the World Golf Hall of Fame in 1997.

SIR NICK FALDO

Nicholas Alexander Faldo has been the most successful British golfer of the modern era. He was born in 1957 in Welwyn Garden City. A natural sportsman he could have picked his sport and would probably have excelled in any but it was actually seeing Jack Nicklaus on television when he was 13 years old that settled the matter for him. Early in his career, having enjoyed success on the tour, he decided that if he was going to win the majors that he craved he would have to improve his swing. Many pundits thought he was making a mistake in trying to tinker with a natural golf swing that clearly worked and which had proven to be successful, and change it for a mechanical one. Yet he did just that and produced a swing that held up under pressure. He went on to win six majors, including three Opens and three Masters titles. In addition he was a brilliant Ryder Cup player and went on to captain the European Ryder Cup team in 2008.

He was inducted into the World Golf Hall of Fame in 1997 and was knighted in 2009.

He has given much back to golf and is involved with academies and golf charities. He is a regular golf commentator in the USA.

BERNHARD LANGER

Bernhard Langer was born in Anhausen in Germany in 1957. He caddied as a youngster and soon demonstrated a mighty talent; with a flattish swing he is one of the most accurate of iron players. Unfortunately, like other great golfers before him, he developed the yips to an extremely damaging extent yet he has overcome them by using different putters and different methods.

He has won many times around the world and has two Masters to his credit. He was also an extremely popular and successful Ryder Cup captain in 2004. He was inducted into the World Golf Hall of Fame in 2001.

GREG NORMAN

Known as the 'Great White Shark' because of his mane of blonde hair and his aggressive brand of golf, Greg Norman is one of the best-known golfers in the world. He was born in Mount Isa, Queensland, Australia. He had many other sporting interests including surfing, so he did not start golf until he was 16. He has won many titles around the world, but his tally of majors does not reflect his talent. He won two Open Championships, but came runner-up in three Masters, two US Opens and two PGAs. Many of his fans felt that bad luck plagued him, or that he seemed so often to be pipped at the post by opponents hitting lucky shots that deprived him of the titles. On all of those occasions, however, he was always gracious in defeat and never made excuses, accepting it as being the game of golf. At the age of 53 he came third in the 2008 Open at Royal Birkdale after having been the third round leader in a championship in which only the good wind players could cope.

Apart from his golf career he is an entrepreneur and has been awarded the Order of Australia. In 2001 he was inducted into the World Golf Hall of Fame.

SANDY LYLE

Sandy Lyle is a Scottish golfer who was born in 1958 in Shrewsbury in England where his father was a golf professional. He has won a Masters and an Open Championship and is held in great affection.

PAYNE STEWART (1957–99)

William Payne Stewart was a much loved and colourful American golfer who dressed in plus twos and coloured sports shirts, in the fashion of golfers of a bygone age. There was nothing bygone about his golf, however. He was a tough competitor who won two US Opens and one PGA.

Tragically, he was killed at the age of 42 when the private aeroplane he was travelling in suffered a catastrophic drop in pressure, killing all aboard.

NICK PRICE

Nicholas Raymond Leige Price was born in Durban in 1957. He is a Zimbabwean citizen and one of the finest international golfers in the world having won three majors, including two PGAs and one Open. He was inducted into the World Golf Hall of Fame in 2003.

IAN WOOSNAM

Ian Woosnam, or 'Woosie' as he is affectionately known, was born in Oswestry in 1958. He won the 1991 Masters and was runner-up in the 1989 US Open. He is small in height, but gifted with magnificent ball-striking and great strength. He was for a while the world number one and was a successful Ryder Cup player and captain.

VIJAY SINGH

Vijay Singh is the most famous and best Fijian golfer of all time. He was born in 1963 and is known as one of the hardest workers on the tour who turned practice into a fine art and profited from the endeavour. He made his name on the European tour first then moved to the PGA tour and started winning majors. He has won the Masters once and also two PGA championships.

He was world number one in 2004 and 2005 and was inducted into the World Golf Hall of Fame in 2005.

COLIN MONTGOMERIE

Colin Montgomerie was born in 1963 and is a great player who has won over thirty titles on the European tour. He was a highly successful Ryder Cup player (unbeaten in singles) and successfully captained the European team to victory in 2010. He won the European Order of Merit a record eight times and was runner-up in five majors.

JOSÉ MARÍA OLAZÁBAL

José María Olazábal was born in Hondarribia in Spain in 1966. He won two Masters and enjoyed a successful Ryder Cup career, partnering Seve Ballesteros. In 2006 he partnered Sergio Garcia.

ERNIE ELS

Theodore Ernest Els – known in the golfing world as 'The Big Easy' because of his almost effortless swing and his laid-back attitude – has been one of the most popular golfers since the 1990s. He is a fierce matchplay golfer who has won the World Matchplay Championship an incredible seven times as well as four majors, including two US Opens and two Opens. He has also been runner-up in the Masters twice.

He was inducted into the World Golf Hall of Fame in 2011.

TIGER WOODS

Eldrick Tont Woods, known to the world as Tiger, was born in Cypress, California, in 1975. He demonstrated natural talent at an incredibly early age to his father, Earl Woods, a Vietnam veteran and a single handicap golfer himself. His prodigious talent quickly gained national interest and his list of golfing feats began in childhood. For example, at the age of 3 he had broken fifty on the Cypress Naval Course.

He played college golf at Stanford University and won the US Amateur three times in a row. In 1996 he turned professional and immediately landed huge endorsement deals. In 1997 he won the Masters, breaking countless records in doing so – he was the youngest player to win, the first African-American, and he won with a record-breaking 18 under par and a lead of twelve shots.

Throughout his career Tiger Woods has attracted huge galleries who came to see him hit colossal distances, conjure up fantastic shots and putt like no-one before him had done. Gradually he notched up major after major, until he had reached fourteen major titles, threatening to overtake the great Jack Nicklaus's record of eighteen titles. To date he has won four Masters, four PGAs, three US Opens and three Open championships.

Beset by injuries and personal problems his winning streak came to an end and he dropped down the rankings from number one in the world. Gradually it looks as if his game is resurfacing and only time will tell whether he will surpass Jack Nicklaus's long-standing record. He is certainly a phenomenal golfer to watch and one suspects that he will return to his major-winning ways.

PHIL MICKELSON

Philip Alfred Mickelson was born in San Diego, California, in 1970. He is one of the most popular golfers in the world, renowned for his ever-ready smile and his great sportsmanship. He is known as 'Phil' or sometimes 'Lefty', because he plays left-handed (although he is right-handed in other aspects of life). He has accumulated a lot of victories, including four majors. For many years he seemed to be in Tiger Woods' shadow, but broke through to reveal his own talents. His short game and putting are sublime, yet he can give the ball 'some pop,' as he refers to it when he hammers it great distances. To date he has won three Masters and one PGA as well as being a successful Ryder Cup player.

In 2012 he was inducted into the World Golf Hall of Fame.

PÁDRAIG HARRINGTON

Pádraig Harrington was born in Dublin in Ireland in 1971 and after a successful amateur career he turned professional in 1995. He has won three majors, including back-to-back Open victories in 2007 and 2008 and the PGA in 2008. He has also been a Ryder Cup player.

GREAT WOMEN CHAMPIONS

Although Mary, Queen of Scots played golf it became frowned upon for women to play in succeeding centuries. It was not really until the nineteenth century that women golfers started to play the game seriously. Even then they had to put up with the social conventions of the day; for example it was suggested that they should not swing above shoulder height since it was unladylike. If they aimed to drive the ball no more than 80 yards then they would not lose decorum. Fortunately there were several champions who threw off such ludicrous restrictions and demonstrated that they could play the sport just as well as the men.

Lady Margaret Scott (1874–1938)
Margaret Scott was the daughter of the 3rd Earl of Eldon. She won the first three British Ladies Amateur Championships in 1893, 1894 and 1895.

Cecil Leitch (1891–1977)
Charlotte Cecilia Pitcairn Leitch, known as 'Cecil', was an extremely talented golfer who won four British Ladies Amateur Championships and possibly could have won more. She won her first in 1914 before the First World War and then won back-to-back titles in 1920 and 1921 when the championship began again. She also famously played Harold Hilton, the great amateur who won the Open twice. She received a shot at alternate holes, and beat him.

Glenna Collett Vare (1903–89)
Glenna Collett Vare was a superb American amateur golfer, winning six US Women's Amateur Championships. She was often referred to as the female Bobby Jones in acknowledgement of her gifted game.

Lottie Dod (1871–1960)
Charlotte Dod, known always as Lottie, was a phenomenal sportsperson. She won five Wimbledon Ladies Singles Championships, then turned to golf and won the 1904 British Ladies Amateur Championship. She also played hockey and won a silver medal in archery in the 1908 London Olympics.

Joyce Wethered (1901–97)

The great Bobby Jones said that Joyce Wethered was the best golfer of either sex that he had ever seen. Her swing was classical and highly effective and she won four British Ladies Amateur Championships as well as the English Amateur Championship eight times. She married and became Lady Heathcoat-Amory and was inducted into the World Golf Hall of Fame in 1975.

Joyce Wethered.

Babe Zaharias (1911–56)

Mildred Zaharias, known as Babe, was another great all rounder. She excelled at athletics, basketball and golf and was a double Olympic gold medallist. She quickly dominated golf and won five majors.

Her nickname is interesting as she was called 'Babe' after Babe Ruth the great baseball player, because she once hit 5 home runs in a baseball game.

Louise Suggs

Mae Louise Suggs was born in Atlanta, Georgia, in 1923. She was a long hitter who so impressed the comedian Bob Hope that he gave her the nickname of Miss Sluggs, because she could really slug it! She garnered eleven majors and is one of an elite group of six women who have won career grand slams.

Mickey Wright

Mary Kathryn Wright was born in San Diego, California, in 1935 and proved to be a complete all-round player who accumulated 82 victories and thirteen majors. She is one of an elite group of six who have won career grand slams.

Kathy Whitworth

Kathy Whitworth was born in 1939 in Monahans, Texas, and was a multiple winner, notching up 88 LPGA victories and six majors. She has won more times than any other female professional golfer.

Jan Stephenson

Jan Stephenson was born in 1951 in Sydney and was one of the finest Australian professional golfers. She won three majors.

Pat Bradley

Pat Bradley was born in Westford, Massachusetts, in 1951. She has won six majors and is the only person to have won three of the four majors in a single year. She has also had a career grand slam.

Her nephew is Keegan Bradley, the 2011 PGA champion.

Juli Inkster

Juli Inkster was born in Santa Cruz, California, in 1960. A terrific competitor she has won seven majors and is also one of the elite group of six who have won career grand slams.

Laura Davies

Laura Davies was born in Coventry in 1963. She has won four majors and is the best female British golfer of her generation.

Nancy Lopez

Nancy Lopez was born in 1957 in Torrance, California. She has won three majors and many more titles on the LPGA tour. She has been a great ambassador for the women's game.

Annika Sörenstam

Annika Sörenstam was born in Stockholm in 1970. She has won all over the world and has accumulated ten majors and numerous honours. She is one of an elite group of six who have won career grand slams. Her game was quite peerless and it was a sad day for the game when she retired.

Karrie Webb

Karrie Webb was born in Ayr, Queensland, Australia, in 1974. In 1996 she became the first player on the LPGA to make more than a million dollars in a season. So far she has won seven majors and has even won a super career grand slam, since she has won five of the majors available. This is because she won the du Maurier Classic in 1999 when it was one of the majors.

Se Ri Pak

Se Ri Pak was born in South Korea in 1977. She has been a prodigious winner and has to date accumulated five majors. She was admitted to the World Golf Hall of Fame in 2007.

Yani Tseng

Yani Tseng was born in Taiwan in 1989 and has also amassed five majors. She has the distinction of being the youngest player, either male or female, to have won five major championships.

8

THE RYDER CUP

'I trust that the effect of this match will be to influence a cordial, friendly and peaceful feeling throughout the whole civilised world . . . I look upon the Royal and Ancient game as being a powerful force that influences the best things in humanity.'
Samuel Ryder (1858–1936)

The Ryder Cup is a biennial competition played between teams of professional golfers from Europe and the USA. It is administered by the PGA of America and the PGA European Tour and the players receive no prize money, but play for the honour of representing their continent. It is the most important team match in the golfing calendar.

BACKGROUND

There is debate among golf historians as to who first came up with the idea of having an international team match between the professional golfers on both sides of the Atlantic. Some aver that it was Sylvanus P. Jermain, the president of the Inverness Club of Toledo, Ohio, while others say that it was James Harnett, a circulation representative of *Golf Illustrated*. Whoever it was managed to spark off enough interest for something to happen. In 1921 a golf match was held at Gleneagles in Scotland between a team of professional golfers from the USA against a team of golfers from Great Britain. It was a win for the British golfers by 10½ points to 4½, but due to lack of funding and lack of enthusiasm another was not played until 1926. The great Walter Hagen was a member of the losing 1921 team. He was, however, extremely keen that such an event should become a regular feature of the golfing calendar. In 1926 another match was held at Wentworth in Surrey, and again the British team won, this time by 13½ to 1½. You might have thought that Hagen would have had enough by then, but not a bit of it.

THE RYDER CUP

Enter Sam Ryder, a 68-year-old millionaire seed merchant from St Albans. Depending upon which source you go to, either at a tea party or a champagne supper with the golfers after the 1926 event he suggested that a match between the two countries should become a regular thing. Hagen was enthusiastic about it, then George Duncan the professional at Wentworth and a player in both 1921 and 1926, challenged Sam Ryder to perhaps put up a trophy as an inducement. The seed was planted, so to speak.

After all the arrangements had been made, a team of British golfers crossed the Atlantic in 1927 on the Cunard liner *Aquitania*. Unfortunately, due to appendicitis Abe Mitchell, Sam Ryder's personal professional, was unable to go. The first official Ryder Cup match was played at the Worcester Country Club in Massachusetts. The format was four foursome matches on the first day and eight singles on the second day, so there were a total of 12 points available. Unlike the previous matches, this was a resounding victory for the USA, with a score of 9½ to 2½.

SAM RYDER

The sponsor of the trophy and of the great international competition that bears his name was Samuel Ryder. The fourth of eight children born to Samuel Ryder Snr, a gardener, and his wife Elizabeth, a dressmaker, Samuel Jnr trained as a teacher in Manchester. However, he never actually took up his calling, since ill health prevented him from taking his final examinations. Instead he worked for his father for a while, who had established a nursery and built up a business as a seed merchant. However, they did not work well together and Samuel Jnr moved to London to work for a rival firm. It was not long before he branched out on his own, thanks to a superb entrepreneurial idea. Essentially, he started a mail order business, selling seeds in small packages for a penny a pack. The business bloomed and he became a wealthy man.

From this he established, along with his brother, a herb growing company, which was called Heath and Heather. This too blossomed and he became wealthier still.

Middle-aged Sam Ryder took up golf and fairly quickly attained a good single figure handicap of six under the tutelage of the renowned golf professional Abe Mitchell, whom he employed as his personal instructor with a salary of £1,000 a year, a substantial income in 1925. In 1910 he was admitted to the membership of Verulam Golf Club in St Albans and a year later he was made club captain.

He was a great advocate of clubs sponsoring young professional golfers and he was passionate about international competition between the best golfers of the USA and Great Britain and Ireland.

He died surrounded by his family during a Christmas holiday at his favourite hotel in London at the age of 77 years.

THE RYDER CUP TROPHY

The trophy has been played for every two years, apart from the Second World War years (1939–45) and after the atrocity of the bombing of the Twin Towers on 11 September 2001. After the latter it has been played on even years.

It is a solid gold cup that was valued at £250 at the time of its design by Mappin and Webb & Co. It features a golfer on its lid, which Sam Ryder insisted should look like his golf instructor and friend, Abe Mitchell.

To win the Ryder Cup a team has to win outright by at least one point while a tied match means that the team who are the holders at the start of that year's competition will retain it.

FORMAT CHANGES

From 1927 to 1959, inclusive, the format was four foursome matches on the first day and eight singles on the second day, with a point available for each match – thus there were 12 points available.

However, in 1961 the format was changed to four foursomes in the morning on the first day with another four foursomes that afternoon. On the second day there were eight singles in the morning and eight singles again in the afternoon, thus the points available were increased to 24 points.

In 1963 the event was expanded to three days. The middle day consisted of eight four-ball matches. This extended the points available to 32. In 1977 five foursomes were played on day one, five four-balls were played on the second day and ten singles on the final day with the points available reduced to 20 points.

In 1979 the competition was extended to include European golfers, so that it became the USA v Europe. The format was extended again, so that four foursomes and four four-balls were played on each of the first two days, followed by twelve singles on the final day. The points available became 28.

RESULTS

The years up to the Second World War saw the USA winning 4 times and Great Britain and Ireland winning twice.

After the Second World War the USA attained dominance, winning 14 times and tying once. Great Britain and Northern Ireland only won once in 1957.

Following the American victory in 1977 there were discussions that led to the inclusion of European golfers into the competition, so that it became USA against Europe. This led to much more competitive matches and a change in the balance of the results. Europe fielded hugely talented players such as Seve Ballesteros, Bernhard Langer, Nick Faldo and the inspirational captain, Tony Jacklin. Since 1979 up to and including 2010 the European side has won 8 times and tied once to retain the cup, against 7 wins and one tie by the USA.

So, things are certainly pretty well balanced now, but up to and including 2010, the USA has still won 25 times out of the 38 times the Ryder Cup has been played. It has only been tied twice, in 1989 when Europe retained it under Tony Jacklin's captaincy and in 1969 when the USA retained it under Sam Snead's captaincy.

TOP SCORERS

Most successful captains

USA	Walter Hagen, captained 6 matches, won 4
	Sam Snead, captained 3, won 3
GB & NI and Europe	Tony Jacklin, captained 4, won 2, tied and retained 1

Most appearances

Sir Nick Faldo	11 matches for GB & NI and Europe

Most points

Sir Nick Faldo	25 points

Most Singles points
All with 7 points:

Colin Montgomerie (Europe)

Billy Casper (USA)

Lee Trevino (USA)

Arnold Palmer (USA)

Neil Coles (GB & NI)

ONE OF THE GREAT SPORTING MOMENTS OF RYDER CUP HISTORY

In the 1969 Ryder Cup at Royal Birkdale, Tony Jacklin and Jack Nicklaus were the two anchormen. Jacklin holed an eagle putt on the 17th to draw level and they came to the last with Jacklin needing to win the hole to win the Ryder Cup. He putted to 2ft while Nicklaus had a 15ft, but raced it 4ft beyond the hole. The putt was too long for Jacklin to concede and Nicklaus duly holed the putt. That meant that Jacklin's 2ft-putt, which was missable, would give the USA a realistic chance of winning the cup outright. Nicklaus, however, was conscious of the weight of expectation that would rest on Jacklin's shoulders. He picked up the marker and handed it to Jacklin, telling him that he did not think he would miss the putt, but he had no intention of giving him the chance.

A truly great sporting moment. It meant that the Ryder Cup was tied, and since the USA had been in possession of the cup at the start, they retained it.

9

THE OTHER MAJOR TEAM MATCHES

'Man is a gaming animal. He must always be trying to get the
better of something or other.'
Charles Lamb (1775–1834),
English essayist

The Ryder Cup is the oldest and the most famous of the team
matches played in golf and as such deserves the following that
it gets. Yet there are several other important team competitions
which may not gain quite as much news coverage but still
provide great spectacles throughout the golfing year.

THE PRESIDENT'S CUP

This is a Ryder Cup equivalent competition played between
professional golfers from the USA against professional golfers
from the rest of the world apart from Europe. It is played in a
similar format with twelve players and a non-playing captain
per team. It was started in 1994 and was played biennially until
the 9/11 atrocity when both the Ryder Cup and the President's
Cup were pushed back a year. It is now played in odd-numbered
years.

As with the Ryder Cup the players receive no prize money, but
play for the honour of their team. All proceeds from the event go
to charity.

Up to and including 2011, there have been 9 competitions –
the USA have won 7 matches and tied once, compared to the
Rest of the World which has won once and tied once.

THE SOLHEIM CUP

This is the Ryder cup equivalent for women professional golfers. It was inaugurated in 1990 and is played in alternate years to the Ryder Cup. The format is the same.

Up to and including 2011 the Solheim Cup has been played 12 times, with the USA winning 8 times and the Europeans 4 times.

THE WALKER CUP

This is the main amateur competition played biennially by a team of the top amateur golfers from the USA against a team from Great Britain and Northern Ireland. Unlike the professional Ryder Cup competition the Walker Cup has not been expanded to include players from Europe. It is co-organised by the R&A and the US Golf Association.

George Herbert Walker, the grandfather and great-grandfather of American presidents George H.W. Bush and George W. Bush respectively, was instrumental in establishing this competition. In 1920 he was the president of the US Golf Association and following discussions about holding an annual international competition a cup was named in his honour. Originally an invitation was sent out by the US Golf Association to all countries to send a team to compete for the cup, but only GB & NI were able to do so. From then on it has only been played by the two sides. An informal match was held in 1921 and then annual matches were played on either side of the Atlantic until 1924. It then became a biennial event, like the Ryder Cup. Since the Second World War it has been played in odd-numbered years.

Up to and including 2011 the USA lead by 34 wins to the GB & NI's 8, with one tied match.

THE CURTIS CUP

This is the main women amateur golfers' team event, played for between the USA and Great Britain and Northern Ireland. It is played by 8 players per team and since the first event in 1932 it has been competed for on alternating sides of the Atlantic in even years apart from during the Second World War.

The trophy is a silver bowl which was donated by the Curtis Sisters, Harriot and Margaret, both of whom had been US Amateur Champions.

The format is similar to that of the Walker and Ryder cups, but with some variations. Up to 2010 it had been played 36 times, the USA winning 28 times and GB & NI winning 8 times.

THE SEVE TROPHY

This is a biennial team event played between professional golfers from Great Britain and Northern Ireland against a team from Europe. It was first called 'The Vivendi Trophy with Seve Ballesteros' in 2009 and then in 2011 was called the 'Vivendi Seve Trophy'. It is a mark of respect to one of the greatest professional golfers.

The teams are chosen according to ranking points on the Official World Rankings and on the European Tour's Race to Dubai. It is played in non-Ryder Cup years and its aim is to give European golfers team golf opportunities to keep players focused for the greater challenge of the Ryder Cup.

OFFICIAL WORLD GOLF RANKING

In 1986 this system was introduced for ranking professional male golfers. It was started because of difficulties experienced in giving out invitations to players for some of the majors. This arose because there are various tours and different professionals play on one or more. By introducing a world ranking system, points could be accrued on the different tours, thereby giving players a world ranking.

The system is quite complex, but includes the four majors and the six main tours:

US PGA tour – based in USA

European tour – based in Europe and UK

Asian tour – based in Asia except Japan

PGA tour of Australasia – based in Australia and New Zealand

Japan tour – based in Japan

Sunshine tour - based in South Africa

High finishes in other tours are included.

THE RACE TO DUBAI

Since 2009 the European Order of Merit has been changed to the Race to Dubai.

10

URBAN GOLF

'It's good sportsmanship not to pick up
lost balls while they are still rolling.'
Mark Twain

I have a recurring nightmare. It usually starts innocuously
enough with me teeing off in a threesome on one or other of my
favourite courses. I usually get off to a good start until I come
to a tee where I inexplicably have to play through a crowded
street. People are milling around, shopping, sitting at street
cafés or waiting to cross the road. There are cars coming and
going. Glass-fronted skyscrapers tower above on both sides of
the street.

'Come on, get a move on!' someone shouts behind me. 'There
are lots of us waiting to play, you know.'

I bend down and tee the ball on the square of grass on the
pavement, my hands visibly trembling.

'Remember all the shops and the office blocks are out of
bounds,' someone reminds me.

'You have to pay for breakages.'

'Twelve stroke penalty if you hit anyone!'

Beads of perspiration form on my brow and I wonder about
putting the ball up the street. It is only a momentary thought that
is swiftly swept aside by the mocking tone of one of my playing
partners.

'You're not chicken, are you?'

He starts to do an imitation of a chicken dance and starts
clucking. Passers by begin laughing, although clearly not at him,
but at me.

I decide to play conservatively and take a 5 iron. If I play a
controlled punch shot and aim for the open street beyond the

bus, I calculate how long the ball will remain in the air and hope that I can time it to land before the taxi and the motorcyclist that have just set off.

I waggle the club a couple of times and will my nerves to settle. Then as I swing the club back I find that it has suddenly turned into a snake-like creature that writhes and clearly dislikes being handled so incompetently. But somehow after a tussle I manage to complete the swing. I connect with the ball and it sails away, up, up and then it turns, and turns, and turns – heading towards . . .

There is the shattering noise of glass. Whole glass-fronted skyscrapers start to crash to the earth.

'You idiot!' someone shouts. 'You're supposed to shout Fore!'

I wake, covered in perspiration, having fallen out of bounds and successfully pulled all of the bedclothes with me. In my thrashing about I have knocked the glass from the bedside table.

'Not again!' I recognise my long-suffering wife's voice.

Urban golf! When I first heard the name I thought it was some sort of sick joke – I could not imagine why on earth anyone would wish to put themselves through the horrors of my nightmare, yet that is precisely what these stalwart folk do. They have literally taken to the streets and staged tournaments all over the place.

People have of course knocked balls around in streets for years. Old Tom Morris apparently first wielded a club by knocking corks weighted with nails around the streets of St Andrews. Yet it is the person who first thought of actually using the streets to simulate a golf course who deserves credit. The late Jeremy Feakes, an architect who tragically died in an accident in 2007 at the age of 34, was the originator of urban golf. Apparently the idea came to him when he was walking through Covent Garden with his clubs. He began asking people if they had seen his ball and their reactions resulted in his eureka moment.

In 2004 he organised the first Urban Open Golf championship and it took place in the streets of Shoreditch in London. There were 63 applicants chosen from over 300 and the event proved immensely popular with events now being held all over the world.

The game is played along the pavements and roads, between designated tees. The balls are reminiscent of the old-fashioned featheries, being leather covers stuffed with cotton rather than feathers. Individual events may use different balls, but the essence is that they will neither injure anyone, nor break any windows.

I have yet to be tempted onto one of these urban fairways, but perhaps it would be a good idea. It could cure my nightmares.

CROSSGOLF

This is an earlier version that is similar, but different. Torsten Schilling began practising near office blocks in his native Germany in 1992. He started a movement called Crossgolf that used car parks, disused building sites and so on, which became Natural Born Golfers.

LONG-DISTANCE GOLF

Between 14 September 1963 and 10 October 1964 Floyd Rood, a golf professional from St Mary's Golf Club not too many miles from New Orleans, drove a golf ball across the USA from the Pacific to Atlantic coast. He covered 3,398 miles in 114,737 strokes, losing 3,511 balls along the way.

THE FIRST PROFESSIONAL URBAN GOLFERS

After the Tijuana Open in 1928 the Australian golfer Joe Kirkwood bet Walter Hagen $50 that he could play his ball back to their hotel in fewer shots. They played the first game of professional urban golf by playing through the streets all the way to the hotel. Kirkwood had played more shots in getting to the hotel, but won the money when he chipped into the toilet bowl, the ultimate target, before Hagen.

11

GOLF IN BOOKS AND FILM

'There is no such thing as a moral or an immoral book.
Books are well written or badly written.'
Oscar Wilde (1854–1900),
The Picture of Dorian Gray

The number of books written about golf every year would be enough to fill Old Tom Morris's shed at St Andrews – it is just as well that he doesn't use it any more.

Golf writing can be divided into four main types. Firstly, instructional pieces most often written by professional golfers for the numerous golf magazines, but with occasional books by amateurs who have discovered the 'golf secret' that will transform the duffer into a scratch player in a couple of rounds.

Secondly, golf journalism, by professional sports writers. These chaps make a significant living by writing regular newspaper and magazine columns interspersed with the odd potboiler book about the latest major or Ryder Cup competition. Thirdly, golf-based travel writing extolling the joys or otherwise of various courses around the world. These are great reads best saved for snowy spells when you have no chance of playing for days on end.

Lastly, there are novels about golf. And I am nuts about them.

Instructional Books

Now these are absolutely addictive. A club professional once told me that he loves all of these books and magazines, because they do him a great service. People buy them, apply them and then screw their games up. After a while they hobble in to see him and apologetically ask for a lesson to put them back on track.

A word of warning, therefore! Consider that you are a unique individual and that the swing thoughts that have been put down on paper by these teachers, many of whom have been champions at the very highest levels, may not work for you. Here is a list of some of the notable instructional guides that have been published over the years.

The Game of Golf, by W. Park Jnr, 1896 – a wonderful description of golf as played in those early days with some good instructional pieces.

The Gate to Golf, by J. Douglas Edgar, 1920 – a superb little book by a golfer who might have achieved true greatness if it hadn't been for his early, tragic death following a vicious knife attack in 1920. He had, however, won the French Open, the Canadian Open twice and the Southern Open. In his book he outlines a simple move that is the secret of great golf. Worth searching out!

Putting Made Easy: the Mark G. Harris Method, by P.A. Vaile, 1935 – an amateur golfer's putting method. Mark Harris did not take golf up until he retired from a successful business.

How to Play Your Best Golf All the Time, by Tommy Armour, 1954 – I admit this is my favourite. The man's personal history makes this irresistible, and he covers everything.

Fontana Golf Book, by Louis T. Stanley, 1957 – I love this old Fontana paperback.

The Golf Secret, by Dr H.A. Murray, 1974 – this is absolutely a classic in the 'secret of golf' genre. When I discovered it back in the 1970s I thought I had discovered gold! But then I always do.

The Lazy Golfer's Companion, by Peter Alliss, 1995 – this is a sort of instructional book for the armchair golfer who doesn't practice a lot. I say 'sort of' since it is peppered with anecdotes in Peter Alliss' inimitable way. Brilliant book.

Ben Hogan's Five Lessons: the Modern Fundamentals of Golf, by Ben Hogan, new edition 2006. Every golfer could benefit from reading this book.

Practical Golf, by John Jacobs, 2005 – an updated version of an earlier work, this man is a teaching genius and I cannot help but recommend anything he writes.

David Leadbetter's Positive Practice: Improve your all-round game, by David Leadbetter, 2005 – a superb book that focuses on golf from many directions, including when you are away from the course. A marvellous book by a top teacher.

Murder on the Links

Golf has been used as a background by crime writers for donkeys' years. In the 1930s and '40s writers could make a decent living by supplying short stories to magazines in all manner of genres from the adventure story to the Western. Golf lends itself to the telling of tales, especially crime stories because of those copses, bushes and bunkers where bodies may be secreted. For the connoisseur of golfing stories there are many that are worth seeking out in the magazines and anthologies of yesteryear. And hopefully, with the profusion of sites on the internet it will not be long before fresh markets for golf tales will open up.

The following are examples of great golf short crime stories worth seeking out:

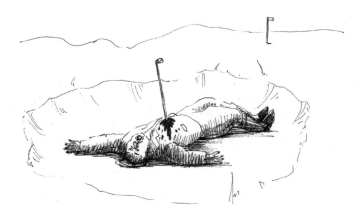

'The Sunningdale Mystery', by Agatha Christie. The whole world knows the name of Agatha Christie, the Queen of Crime. This story is one of her Tommy and Tuppence stories that appears in the anthology *Partners in Crime* and is about the finding of the body of a Captain Anthony Sessle, who has been stabbed through the heart with a hatpin on the 7th tee at Sunningdale Golf Club. It is vintage Christie. It first appeared in the *Sketch* magazine on 22 October 1924. It appeared there as the *Sunninghall Mystery*, but was published in the anthology of short stories *Partners in Crime* in 1929 as 'The Sunningdale Mystery'.

'Murder in the Mews', by Agatha Christie. This is a long short story written by Agatha in 1937 and is a delightful locked-room murder mystery. The golf element is fundamental to the plot and it is great fun to try to solve this one. The course Agatha used on this occasion was Wentworth.

'The Murder on the Golf Links', by M. McDonnell Bodkin. This writer is all but forgotten today but Mathias McDonnell Bodkin was a barrister, judge and MP for North Roscommon in Ireland. While not being as prolific as Agatha Christie, he nonetheless notched up a respectable 39 publications which included many novels and countless short stories. He introduced two detectives, Paul Beck and Dora Myrl, who had their own adventures before marrying and having a son, who also became a detective. This story is a delightful golfing mystery with a twist to match any blind dogleg on your own golf course.

Novels of Golf

There are a huge number of novels that are golf-based. The older ones come replete with the archaic names, the different rules and many of them may seem dated for the modern taste. However, they are often quite interesting social commentaries and should be read with their period in mind. Here are some enjoyable reads:

Murder at the Open, by Angus MacVicar, 1965. I start with this tale of murder at the Open, because it was set in St Andrews and I have always been fond of the tales by Angus MacVicar (1908–2001). He was a prolific children's writer from South Uist.

Trent's Own Case, by Edmund Clerihew Bentley, 1936. This is a comic detective crime novel that Bentley wrote to follow on from his classic novel *Trent's Last Case*. In it Phillip Trent, an amateur criminologist and artist, finds himself connected to the murder of a philanthropist, James Randolph, whose portrait he had been painting.

His golf prowess is highly relevant to the tale.

Bentley also wrote *The Sweet Shot* in 1939 in which a murder is committed using an exploding golf ball!

Goldfinger, by Ian Fleming, 1959. The golf match between James Bond and Auric Goldfinger is beautifully described (and memorably shot in the film of the same name starring Sean Connery). A couple of points about it are worth noting. Firstly, James Bond plays with a hickory-shafted putter that he calls Calamity Jane, just as did the great Bobby Jones. Secondly, Goldfinger putts in 'the new fashion – between his legs with a mallet putter.' This was a new method that Sam Snead had devised to help him over the yips in his later career. It was, unfortunately, outlawed by the USGA.

The Secret of Bogey House, by Herbert Adams, 1924. This is one of several golfing mysteries written by Herbert Adams (1874–1958). They really are quite dated now, but Adams was a clever writer and if you enjoy period crime fiction, these are worth seeking out. He also wrote *The Body in the Bunker* (1935), *Death off the Fairway* (1936), *Nineteenth Hole Mystery* (1939) and *Death on the First Tee* (1957).

Hole in One, by Catherine Aird, 2005. This is the twentieth novel in Catherine Aird's Inspector Sloane series. It is a cosy murder novel by one of the UK's top crime writers. A body is found in dreaded Hell's Bunker.

Death is a Two-Stroke Penalty, by James Bartlett, 1991. I was really happy when I discovered James Bartlett's books about his hero Pete Hacker who has to solve the murder of an obnoxious rising star who is found dead underneath his golf cart.

Bartlett has also written *Death from the Ladies Tee* in 1992 and *Death at the Member-Guest*, in 2004.

Backspin, by Harlan Coben, 1997. This novel features Myron Bolitar, a New York sports agent who goes on the trail of the kidnapped son of a golf star. It's rollercoaster stuff taking you back to a major championship from decades ago and which shows you that golf is not a gentle game.

The Art of Coarse Golf, by Michael Green, first published in 1967 and printed repeatedly since then, is one of the funniest books on golf ever. I split my sides with laughter when I first read it, having only recently taken the game up. It is still uproariously funny.

The Golf Omnibus, by P.G. Wodehouse, 1973. This hilarious collection of golf tales about the idle rich comes from the pen of the most gifted comedy writer of the twentieth century. Many of the stories are narrated by the Oldest Member. This genial chap sits in a corner of the clubhouse or on the veranda, ever-ready to give unfortunate members the benefit of an anecdote or two. Where the club is, it is hard to say. It could be any club, actually, even yours.

I mention the 'Magic Plus Fours' in the chapter on Golf Psychology, but among the splendid stories in this omnibus are 'Ordeal by Golf', 'The Awakening of Rollo Podmarsh', 'The Clicking of Cuthbert' and 'There's Always Golf'. If you are a true golfer these gems will have the tears rolling down your cheeks.

Missing Links, by Rick Reilly, 1996. This is a great American humorous novel about four buddies who live outside Boston and who play on a down-market course, but aspire to play on the neighbouring blue chip one. More laughs per hole than you thought possible.

GOLF AT THE MOVIES

After reacquainting myself with all of those wonderful golf books how could I ignore some of the wonderful films about golf that have been made over the years.

It is going to be a short list, but only because there are so many that I can only give you what I consider to be the top eleven that you may enjoy seeing.

Convict 13

This was a silent movie directed in 1920 by Buster Keaton, starring Buster Keaton and written by Buster Keaton (and Eddie Cline).

It is about an inept golfer who, while following a pretty girl on a golf course trying to impress her, manages to knock himself out by ricocheting a ball off the wall of a shed. An escaped convict discovers him, swaps clothing and makes off. When he regains consciousness Keaton resumes his game of golf, but attracts the attention of a positive army of guards from the prison, because of the prison clothing. Then follows a typical silent movie chase which ends by Keaton going into the prison. Once there the antics continue and he discovers that the pretty girl golfer is actually the warden's daughter. More than that, the prisoner whose uniform he is wearing – Convict 13 – is due to be hanged that day.

It is a frenetic action movie with lots of violence, but Keaton foils a prison breakout and gets the girl. Or rather she gets him in the little twist ending.

The Idle Class

This was a silent movie written and directed by Charlie Chaplin in 1921. It features Chaplin in two roles, one as a feckless, rich alcoholic and the other as the little tramp that the world got to know and love.

The little tramp goes for a round of golf, creating his usual balletic havoc. Edna Purviance, one of his frequent leading ladies, plays a neglected wife and Mack Swain plays her father. For Chaplin fans who like a bit of golf this is sheer delight.

Pat and Mike

This is a 1952 romantic comedy starring Katharine Hepburn and Spencer Tracy and it was directed by George Cukor.

Pat Pemberton, played by Katharine Hepburn, is a multi-talented sportswoman who is a champion in various sports (the role was specially written for Hepburn who was adept herself at tennis and golf). In the film, the problem is that she has a domineering fiancé who does not appreciate her talents and when he is around she goes to pieces, losing the Ladies Golf Championship as a result. Then along comes Mike, a shady golf promoter, played by Spencer Tracy. She wants to win and he takes her under his wing, causing all manner of dodgy situations to arise.

The Caddy

This is a 1953 movie directed by Norman Taurog, featuring Jerry Lewis and Dean Martin. Harvey Miller Jnr (Lewis) is a gifted golfer, but he is too shy and nervous to play in front of people. He coaches and caddies for his girlfriend's brother Joe Anthony (Martin). Joe has to be a success at golf to stop his fisherman father from making him spend his life at sea. In a sense, they are at sea on the links.

Goldfinger

This 1964 movie was the third James Bond film featuring Sean Connery and it was based on the 1959 novel by Ian Fleming. Directed by Guy Hamilton and produced by Albert (Cubby) Broccoli, the film sees villain, Auric Goldfinger, played by Gert Fröbe, plan to break into Fort Knox with the help of Pussy Galore (Honor Blackman), and her Flying Circus.

The golf match that Ian Fleming so meticulously describes in the novel is altered so that Goldfinger's Korean manservant Oddjob, played by Harold Sakata, brings his own style of caddying to the game – it's a perfect needle match.

Caddyshack

This hilarious spoof on golf made in 1980 was written by Brian Doyle-Murray, Douglas Kenney and Harold Ramis, and directed by Harold Ramis. It stars Chevy Chase, Rodney Dangerfield, Ted Knight, Michael O'Keefe, Cindy Morgan and Bill Murray (who is terrific as a greenkeeper who takes his job perhaps a little too seriously).

Tin Cup

This is a 1996 romantic comedy directed by Ron Shelton, starring Kevin Costner and Rene Russo. Costner plays Roy 'Tin Cup' McAvoy, a gifted but totally unambitious golf professional who has chosen to fritter his life away on his golf range in Texas rather than seek the heights on the tour.

Dr Molly Griswold, played by Rene Russo is a clinical psychologist who wants to learn how to play golf. Inevitably there is an attraction betwixt the two and they each have the ability to solve the other's problems.

Roy decides to try to qualify for the US Open, which he does. If you want to know what happens next, see the film. Do you think I'm the sort of person to ruin your fun?

Happy Gilmore

This is a 1996 comedy directed by Dennis Dugan and starring Adam Sandler about a rejected hockey player, Happy Gilmore, who turns his hand to golf in order to save his grandmother's house (he has to find the money to redeem the property that the bank is threatening to sell). Happy only discovers he has a golfing talent by chance. He has a phenomenally powerful shot and from there the movie takes off.

The Legend of Bagger Vance

This movie made in 2000 was based on the novel by Steven Pressfield, was directed by Robert Redford and stars Will Smith, Matt Damon and Charlize Theron.

It is set in Georgia during the depression after the First World War and revolves around Rannulph Junuh, a prodigiously talented Southern golfer, and his match with Walter Hagen, played by Bruce McGill, and Bobby Jones, played by Joel Gretsch. Junuh (Matt Damon) is aided by the angelic Bagger

Vance (Will Smith) who understands everything about golf and about life, seemingly because he is an angel, and offers philosophical tips in abundance as he caddies and coaches Junuh to success.

The Aviator

This is a 2004 biographical film about the multi-millionaire aviator and movie producer, Howard Hughes, directed by Martin Scorsese. It has a huge cast of prominent actors who play many of the glamorous movie folk of the twenties to the forties.

There is a terrific golf game between Howard Hughes, played by Leonardo DiCaprio, and Katharine Hepburn, played by Cate Blanchett. Hepburn is wooed by Hughes and lives with him for a while, until she falls in love with Spencer Tracy (with whom she starred in the other golf movie *Pat and Mike*). Cate Blanchett played the role very convincingly, having taken up golf and tennis like Hepburn in order to do so.

The Greatest Game Ever Played

This 2005 movie is based on the true story of the 1913 US Open at Brookline, Massachusetts, where the 20-year-old Francis Ouimet defeated Harry Vardon and Ted Ray in a play-off. It was directed by Bill Paxton and starred Shia LaBeouf as Francis Ouimet. The screenplay was written by Mark Frost, based on his earlier best selling novel.

This is a feel-good biographical movie and through little vignettes it tells about Harry Vardon and his growth into the great golfer that he was, struggling against social class, just as Ouimet did. It was, after all, a time when golf was a game played by the wealthy and the professional was not considered worthy to enter the clubhouse.

12

PUTTING

'The man who can putt is a match for any man.'
Willie Park Jnr (1864–1925)

Golf is a game of two parts. The first is the game of getting the ball from the tee to the green but the second is much harder – it is the business of putting into the hole.

Putting! It is a strange word, don't you think? Some suggest that it is derived from the Dutch verb *putten*. Why anyone should think that is beyond me, since it means to draw water from a well. Perhaps it was because missed putts so often turned golfers to tears and drew the water well down their cheeks. Do you buy that? No, nor do I. Personally I think it is more likely to be from good old Scots dialect, and I speak as a man born and bred in the Kingdom of Fife. I can well imagine some aged Fife golfer giving advice to his opponent. 'Ach, just putt it in the hole.'

THE COMING OF THE PUTTER

Back in the old days when greens were simply sheep-nibbled areas of fairway with a hole dug into them somewhere, putting was a different activity. The greens were not specially tended areas but places where the grass seemed to be shorter. Indeed, Willie Park Jnr refers to the rules of golf of his day, stating that the green is defined as the ground within twenty yards of the hole, excepting hazards. Prior to that it seems that often the whole course was referred to as the green. Remember also that in the original game there was no teeing area either. You holed out then drove off from somewhere within a club length of the hole; not exactly the right conditions to maintain a smooth lawn like area.

*Putting can drive a
player to distraction.*

All manner of clubs were used by the early golfers to get the featherie ball into the hole, such as the putting cleek that I mentioned in chapter 4 on clubs. Robert Browning in his excellent book *A History of Golf* says that most golfers in those halcyon days probably had two putters, one called a driving putter for keeping the ball down low when playing on the fairway, and a green-putter when you were getting close to the hole. Indeed, some golfers probably had no proper designated putting utensil, but just used whatever felt right for the job of scuttling the ball towards and eventually into the hole.

As greens became more sophisticated and as greenkeepers started to live up to their names by deliberately contouring the ground, cutting the grass this way or that way and ensuring that no weeds were ever encountered on them, then the need of good honest putters specifically designed for the job became necessary. The only trouble was, what sort of a club was that? You don't have to have been playing golf for long to realise that putting is difficult and getting a putter that is just right for you is somewhat like searching for the Holy Grail. The more profane among the golfing fraternity might say it was a heck of a lot harder.

LET'S KEEP IT SIMPLE

Most of the early golf pros also made clubs. There was not much science involved, more a bit of what seemed right. The great Willie Park Jnr, winner of the Open in 1887 and 1889, invented a 'putting-cleek' which had a bend in the neck just above the blade. In his book *The Game of Golf* he describes how he came to develop it. A total accident, it seems.

> The idea occurred to me during practice for a tournament, when I happened to be with a cleek that had a shaft slightly bent over. I observed that in putting with this cleek the balls seemed to run with more accuracy than usual, and, following up the idea, the patent putter was produced. It is difficult to explain the principle of this club. With an ordinary putter the stroke is of the nature of a push, while with this patent it is more a pull than a push. It also has the advantage of allowing the player to see the blade of the cleek while addressing the ball, as the line of the shaft is in front of the blade. Although I run the risk of being accused of partiality for my own patents, I cannot refrain from saying that I find I can putt much better with this club than with any other I have hitherto tried, and I have received testimonials in its favour from many of the best players of the day, both amateur and professional.

An early putting club

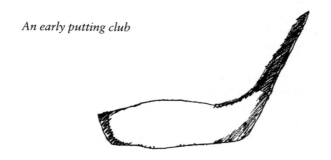

We could go on forever about the putters that have been developed over the years and you only have to walk into any golf pro's shop to see a weird and wonderful collection of implements that only vaguely resemble one another. And when you watch the pros play they seem to be every bit as confused as we ordinary mortals. It seems that matches, tournaments and championships are often won because someone is not only playing superbly well, but they have discovered for the three or four days what is described as a 'hot putter'. Jack Nicklaus won his memorable last major, the 1986 Masters while playing with a putter that had a blade more like an iron girder than a precision tool while Bernhard Langer has been seen playing with a putter that had a succession of golf balls attached behind it, presumably in order to give an impression of how the balls should leave the putter face. Ken Brown used to play with an old hickory-shafted putter that he kept in his bag wrapped up in an old woollen stocking. They all seemed to work for a while and then were abandoned – all, that is, except for Ken Brown's old hickory, which he used to wield so well.

Perhaps we are drifting off into the psychology of putting sooner than I had intended, so let's try to keep it simple. The following are the basic types of putter you will see:

Centre-shafted putter – the shaft is connected into the top of the blade rather like a mallet.

End-shafted putter – the traditional putter, like a cleek.

Long putter – there are really two of these: the broomstick, which players anchor under their chin and play with a pushing pendulum movement, and the belly putter which is longer than a traditional putter and is anchored into or just under the belly button and played otherwise like a traditional putter.

Straight-forward putter – this has not yet caught on in the UK but is seen more frequently in the USA. It is a combination of the mallet putter and the long putter. It is designed so that the player faces the target and putts it in a side-saddle manner, rather as Sam Snead did, but from an upright position using the length of the long shaft.

I LOVE MY PUTTER

The great Bobby Jones could putt the fleas off a dog. He loved his putter and called it Calamity Jane. I have no idea what he called his dog.

James Bond, otherwise known as 007, also used a hickory-shafted putter, which he called Calamity Jane in *Goldfinger*.

Bobby Locke, the winner of the Open in 1949, 1950, 1952 and 1957, was a phenomenal putter. In one year he played 100 rounds of golf and never three-putted once. So enamoured was he with his putter than he occasionally slept with it. It was purely platonic love, of course.

PUTTING ABILITY

It is actually fascinating to find out what people have believed about putting over the years.

Willie Park Jnr had quite marked views; he felt strongly that putting should be the part of the game that everyone should aim to excel in. After all, as he said, a stroke is defined as 'any movement of the club which is intended to strike the ball'. He went on to say that a drive of a couple of hundred yards and a putt of six inches equally count a stroke, notwithstanding the disparity of distance. A few missed putts here and there mean the difference between a good and a bad score. Two strokes on each green were, he felt, the proper allowance for a first class player. It is a truism today as much as back then – if you want to cut shots then the easiest route is by becoming a more proficient putter.

Ah, but there is the rub, you see. Not everyone can putt well. Or at least that has been the opinion shared by many people over the years. Even the greatest golfers have subscribed to that woeful attitude.

The five times Open champion J.H. Taylor actually felt that you had only to look at some of the top professionals to see that this had to be the case, since many of them were poor putters, and if they could not solve the problem of how to putt then how could an amateur expect to.

In his book *Taylor on Golf*, he actually goes on to say:

> After the fair amount of proficiency has been acquired in the
> use of the cleek, iron and mashie, we have the difficulty of the
> putting to surmount. And here I may say at once it is an absolute
> impossibility to teach a man how to putt.

Goodness, if that was what one of the greatest golfers of all
time thought about putting then surely it is a forlorn cause? He
actually later emphasised the point by saying:

> Putting, in short, is so different to any other branch of the game
> that the good putter may be said to be born, not made.

He was not alone among the Great Triumvirate in that belief.
James Braid said much the same thing in his book as did Harry
Vardon, six times Open champion in his book *The Complete
Golfer*.

> I believe seriously that every man has a particular kind of putting
> method awarded to him by nature, and when he putts exactly in
> this way he will do well, and when he departs from his natural
> system he will miss the long ones and the short ones too.

Now if we were to accept the *argumentum ad verecundiam*, the
argument of authority, there would surely be little point in trying
to improve one's putting. Yet simple logic tells us that this cannot
be the case; professional golfers pay colossal amounts of money
to putting gurus to help them nip and tuck their putting styles.
At the very top of the game this is understandable, since they
play for astronomical sums of money.

So what about the ordinary mortal, the amateur club or non-
club golfer? Should he try to get better? Of course he or she
should. Yet few do try to do it properly. Teaching pros spend
a lot of time on the swing and the use of various clubs, but
they are less likely to be asked to help with a player's putting
stroke. It seems that people just feel that they can get on and
do it themselves; they accept that they have good days and bad
days on the greens, just as they hear the pros report when they

are interviewed on television. You often hear the pros say that it was a day that they could not even buy a putt. They mean that for some extraordinary reason their putts just kept lipping out or rolling just too short or just too long.

Most golfers will be aware of this phenomenon – either their putting eye is in or it is out. Some accept it as part of the game; others will dredge up all manner of excuses.

It may be the green's or the greenkeeper's fault – greenkeepers of course come in for a lot of stick. They are castigated for overwatering, underwatering, unevenly watering the greens, or for excessive spiking, or failing to train the worms to put their worm casts anywhere else but on the greens. And very often they are cursed for putting the hole in some stupid position on the green.

Some golfers may just blame the golfing gods, for many golfers are a bit superstitious, even if they won't admit it. What these deities look like is anyone's guess but one imagines that they wear plus fours and play endless games of blissful sub-par golf on celestial courses, taking time to oversee the games of mortals after they have finished their own rounds. Perhaps it is when one of their putts lips out that they send the invisible lightning bolts that diverts the path of the mortal golfer's ball en route to the hole.

SOMETIMES YOU JUST HAVE TO GIVE UP

In 1890 A.J. Lewis took 156 putts on a single green at a golf club in Sussex – and picked it up in frustration, having failed to get it in the hole.

EVEN PROFESSIONALS HAVE FRESH AIR PUTTS

Every golfer will at some stage miss a tap-in. Andrew Kirkaldy lost the 1889 Open at Musselburgh with a fresh-air putt when about to tap in a ball that had stopped on the edge of the hole while Hale Irwin lost the 1983 Open at Royal Birkdale when he fresh-aired a tap-in.

Harry Vardon had a fresh-air putt on the last hole at the 1900 US Open at the Chicago Golf Club. Fortunately he was far enough ahead of the field and the only thing that suffered was his pride.

SO HOW CAN YOU IMPROVE YOUR PUTTING?

I am not a golf professional so you may wonder at my temerity in writing a piece about how to play a particular part of the game. My reason, quite simply is because putting is an area where people flounder, even the pros. The occasional golfer flounders most and really it is to this golfer that I address this section, although others may find it of some value.

What do I mean by the occasional golfer? Well simply the golfer who doesn't play very often or who has long breaks from the game and then effectively practices their game on the course. They may not have played for three months, suddenly get asked to play and so roll up at the course, get the bag out of the car boot and stride onto the tee. Their first practice swing for three months may be the swing immediately before they drive off (I am sure that there will be lots of people who will relate to this). How the game goes may seem to be a matter of luck, depending on that first shot. Then, when they eventually get to the green, the first putt is their first putt for three months and it is likely that it will reflect the errant drive. It is liable to be off line and short and if the first few holes are putted in regulation they have done really well.

The thing is that putting is so vitally important in the game that it is the bit that you definitely should practice before you play. Better to spend time on the practice green than heading to the range to get that drive sorted out. Your aim after a lay-off with the long shots should just be to get it in play so that you have a decent opportunity to make the green in regulation.

DON'T GET FLASHY ON THE GREEN

Andy Bean lost the 1983 Canadian Open by nonchalantly putting with the handle rather than the blade of his putter. He was penalised two shots, the number of shots that he lost by.

THE THREE IMPORTANT ASPECTS OF PUTTING

The stroke

Reading the green

Distance control

These are of equal importance, but most amateur golfers are quite vague about them. They tend to lay greatest emphasis on feel and touch; if they seem to have it right they accept it as being how their game should be. If they don't have it they think their game was just off that day. That is of course the amateur approach that will keep the golfer in the upper handicaps. All good golfers have an ability to score well even when they are not playing well; they do it because they have a strategy working for them. They may not give it such label, for it may be an unconscious strategy.

Consider my old friend Glen Dullan and I. He and I were students together, then house surgeons. We played intermittently because of the pressures of work and the vagaries of being on call, and when we did get out on the course we both accepted that we would not be likely to score well, ergo, we didn't. On the green we would tend to go up to the ball, perhaps wipe any mud off it, then cursorily line it up and then putt. Three-putts were not uncommon. Glen occasionally had a four-putt and even on one very bleary day after he had been up all night assisting at an operation, he seven-putted.

Now that wasn't because of the Yips but was a combination of tiredness and incompetence. You see, he accepted that he was a shambolic and abysmal golfer. He often putted short, and I mean really short! He could putt a 20ft putt 10ft, a 5ft putt 3ft, and I won't even give the number of times he whiffed it or fresh-aired a putt on the edge of the hole.

Not that I was much better. Not then, because we were not really serious about it. Yet it struck me as peculiar that two chaps who could make a decent incision on someone's abdomen and perform some pretty precise procedures (that you don't really need to know about) could go onto a golf course and putt like incompetent hula-hoopers – that is, send it in any direction and rarely manage to keep it going to the hole. I have to emphasise that Glen Dullan went on to become an extremely good surgeon. His golf still stinks, however.

As for me, I left surgery and sought a less chaotic life which would give me more time for things like writing and playing golf. Not that I play a great deal, but I wanted to advance a little up the golfing ladder and feel that I could play with people without the embarrassment of three- and four-putting. So, when I eventually had more time I started thinking about what sort of strategies I could use to make me less incompetent on the greens and I discovered enough to make me a half-decent putter, even when I have long gaps between games.

WHAT I WASN'T DOING RIGHT

The first thing was totally obvious when I compared how I putted with any of the tournament pros. I didn't really pay any attention to reading the green; I certainly didn't prowl about the green, holding my putter like a plumb-bob, and then take umpteen practice putts before addressing the ball and gently stroking it towards the target.

The thing is that I was always conscious of not holding play up. That included my playing partner and the players coming along behind and I had always felt slightly foolish if I pranced about like that, especially when I played off a high handicap at that time. So, rather like most other golfers of my ilk, I just went up to the ball, eyeballed the line from behind the ball and then putted. The results as I have already described were generally abysmal, only on good days reaching the standard of reasonable.

The other thing was I had a variable putting technique. Sometimes a wide stance, sometimes narrow. At times I stood closed, but more usually I was open. I varied the grip, I put my right index finger down the shaft, I kept my right elbow close to my torso, and all manner of other things that I either read about or was advised to try by better putters. Sometimes they worked for a while, and then a run of poor putts would get me tinkering again – that was what the pros never do, they don't tinker on the course. They adopt one stance, one method and they stick with it for the whole round.

PRACTICE

This is fundamental, of course. The thing is that most people have no real idea what they are practising – they imagine that they are practising their stroke, and they do it by simply going out on the practice green, their own lawn or the living room carpet at night and hit balls to a target. That is practice, of course, but is it disciplined? Is it done with any set plan other than hitting the target or getting the ball in the hole? You may think that that is all there is to it, but without a clear idea of what you are doing you will only ever be a touch or feel putter. That may be OK, but it does make you more open to more times when the feel or the touch desert you. It is far better, I think, to have a clear idea of what you are practising.

A REGULAR PUTTING STROKE

When you think about it, it is obvious. The reason most putters are erratic is for the reasons I have just alluded to. They do not have a regular putting stroke, but change their posture and technique all the time.

I decided that I would develop a putting strategy that I would stick to and which I could use instantly, no matter how long between lay-offs from the game. By doing that I would eliminate the variability that I brought to the putting green.

START WITH THE PUTTING EYE

This is very important. Which eye do you putt with?

We met the great Tommy Armour Snr earlier. As you may recall he lost his sight during the First World War after a mustard gas attack and regained sight in his right eye. It was only then that he took up golf and went on to become one of the greatest of his day. Certainly he was always hailed as the greatest iron player. He did not consider himself a great putter, but he clearly was good enough to win three majors and obviously used one eye to great effect.

Many golfers do not realise that they should putt with their dominant eye. This is actually very important and you should test which is your dominant eye, because not doing so could be a reason why a golfer putts less well than they should. Two-thirds of the population are right-eye dominant. Most of them are also right-handed, although not necessarily. There is a simple test to check: extend one arm and make a circle with your forefinger and thumb. View a distant object through this circle, keeping both eyes open. Then alternately close one eye without moving your head or the hand. The object will appear to stay in the centre of the circle with your dominant eye, yet be outside it with the non-dominant one.

Another check can be done with an empty toilet roll tube. Put a ball on the ground and stand over it with the toilet tube in hand and look at the ball through the tube, again keeping both eyes open. Now close your left eye. If the ball is still visible in the tube you are right-eye dominant. And standing with the dominant eye over the ball, that is the position that you need to be in when you putt.

TAKE THE STANCE

This is again something that people do in a vague manner. Yet just as with the main game of golf your aim should be to get into a set-up so that you have the best chance of making a repeatable swing, you also want to be able to make a repeatable putting stroke.

Put a ball on the ground and select a target about 5ft away (the length doesn't matter too much). Look at the ball from behind, actually squatting down and looking at the lie of the putt. You really want to select a straight flat lie, so don't use one that has a break in either direction – this includes your carpet!

Place your putter flat on the ground behind the ball so that its face is at perfect right angles to the target.

Imagine a line extending from the front edge of the ball parallel with the face of the putter. Place your left foot so that the inside of the foot is on that parallel line. I position the front of my shoe exactly four inches back from the ball. I can visualise that distance exactly, but you may choose a variation. The thing is to get the distance that suits you after a bit of practice, then stick with that forever after. Place the right foot either parallel with the left foot or slightly back to be slightly closed.

Put your dominant eye over the ball. You can check the line the ball needs to travel along.

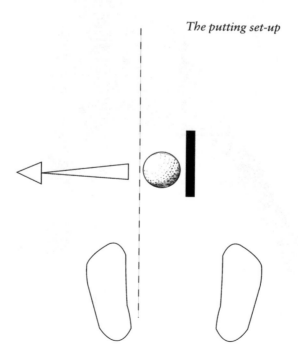

The putting set-up

Holding the putter, ensuring that the putter face is still at right angles to the target line and that the inside of your foot is parallel to the putter face, you are almost ready to putt.

Slightly rotate your left elbow (assuming you are a right-handed putter) so that it is pointing parallel with the target line. This helps to maintain a nice crisp pendulum motion, which is what is needed to avoid deviation of the putter face. Then, putt.

That, I believe is a way of producing a repeatable putt off the left foot. The great amateur golfer Johnny Laidlay, who won the Amateur Championship in 1889 and 1891, always putted off an exaggerated left foot stance. He was considered by Willie Park Jnr one of the greatest putters of his day.

Johnny Laidlay's putting stance

By total contrast, Young Tom Morris putted with an exaggerated open stance, with the ball played off the right heel.

I would not recommend either stance, partly because you do not wish to look too eccentric, but also because it does not give you any landmarks like the position of the foot that I have just described. Yet I think that putting from the left foot (Laidlay putted off the left heel really, as you can see in the picture opposite) is the right position to adopt because you can get the dominant eye over the ball.

BACK TO PRACTICE

The adoption of the stance and the elbow pointing will offer the occasional golfer a set-up that will be consistent. You thereby reduce a lot of the deviations that will creep into the putting stroke when you just depend on feel. It is unashamedly geometric and formulaic, but that is what this aspect of the game needs. You may not turn into a great putter, but you will turn into a consistent one. The more you practice, the more you will become grooved and the more adept you will become. It is a sure way for you to shave strokes from your round.

Now when you practice you should have specific aims, not just loose ones to see how you seem to be putting. One thing that is worth doing is selecting a smaller target than a hole. Use a tee in the ground and putt to that. That really is a superb thing to do to sharpen your putting.

Or toss down say four or five balls so that they are scattered a few feet apart, then putt one ball to strike another. If you miss it, then putt from where it stops until you do hit it. You should never take more than two strokes. Then remove one ball from the game and putt the other one to hit another ball, and then remove another one and so on.

Aiming at a small target is good psychology, because you have a definite aim, rather than a hole to fall into. When you come back to putting at the hole it will look bigger and easier to hit. With the several balls putting exercise your aim should be to hit each ball and do it in the least number of strokes. That also is good psychology.

And even if you are not intending golfing for a long time, practising putting at night on the carpet can be one of the best things you do for your game.

ASSESS DISTANCE

If you are like me and never bothered to find out how far your ball was from the flag then you are definitely missing a trick. A pro will always know exactly how far they are putting. You should always walk the distance of the putt before you take your stance. If you have walked it, walked round it, you have set your brain the task of computing how hard to stroke your putt. It is a subliminal thing, but very important.

And you should practice this when you go on the practice green – assess how accurate you are at judging distance.

PRACTICE DIFFERENT LENGTH PUTTS

So many people go on the practice ground and use it like a seaside putting green, starting at hole 1 and doing a putting round. That is fine if the green is busy, but if you have the opportunity try putting outwards. Start with a 1ft putt, then a 2ft and then a 3ft and so on. Go up as far as you can until you miss one, then start again. You have to aim to get to a certain number before you are happy. It really is a good way of getting the sense of distance.

Another good exercise to help develop that sense is to try a couple of putts from 3ft, then 6ft, then 9ft and then 12ft, two balls each time, aiming for as low a score as possible. Again, good psychology rather than vaguely trying to get the feel. Then try it again, but this time putting one ball, then the second time putting with your eyes closed. Go through the process of getting your stance sorted then close your eyes and putt. It is very good for developing the sense of pace for distance.

READ THE GREENS

The contour of the green will determine where you are aiming your putt – you need to know if the putt is going to break to the right or the left. That basically is what you need to determine so that you can mentally build up a picture of how the ball will roll. Obviously if it is a flat putt then you are going to have to putt straight at the target. If there is a break you have to aim slightly one way or the other to allow for that break. To get that sense you need to get down and have a good look at the lie of the green – do it from behind, then walk round, which gives you the length, and look from behind the hole as well.

Do not worry about how long this takes, since you need to do it to do the job correctly. You can do it quickly, just be sure to do it.

Very importantly, consider how different an uphill putt is from a downhill one – an uphill putt breaks less than a downhill while a downhill putt breaks more than a level or uphiller.

This means that uphill putts can be struck with less allowance for break than a downhiller, and vice versa.

You should also be aware of the grass. The length of the grass will be relevant. If it is longer, then the putts will roll slower than on a finely cut green. Similarly, moisture will slow the ball down.

KNOW WHERE THE SWEET SPOT IS

The sweet spot is the most important part on the face of the putter, as it is with every club. You should hit the ball with it to get the most accurate and true putt. If you don't then you will cause the blade to deviate so that you will hit both right and left of the hole.

The easiest way to find the sweet spot is to hold the putter by the shaft just above the blade so that the blade is horizontal and facing upwards. Then take a ball and slowly just let it bounce on the blade. Keep doing that all the way along. You will be aware of a juddering until you hit the sweet spot when it feels nice and crisp. With a pencil mark the top of the blade so that you can see it when you take up your putting stance. Use that point to hit the middle of the ball.

Finally, always aim to be long rather than short. Remember the adage never up never in.

13

CHIPPING

'In all approach play remember the motto, "Be up," unless there is some good reason to the contrary.'
Willie Park Jnr (1864–1925)

If accuracy and consistency with the putter is the best way for the occasional golfer to reduce his or her score, the second has to be through competence at chipping. Hopefully, you will not need to chip as many as 18 times in a round, but when you do, your aim is to knock it dead so that you only have a short putt afterwards. Occasionally, you will hole one as well.

The chip shot is also referred to as the approach run, or the run-up. It is essentially a shot played from anywhere up to 30 or 40 yards from the flag. It is a standard shot on links courses and surprisingly, is rather disparaged by a lot of golfers who prefer to pitch a shot in simply because they have seen professionals do it so adeptly. Yet the chip is easier to play than the pitch and it is harder to fluff it.

This was another area of my game that I decided to improve upon, if for no other reason than that the short game is so important. I am sure you will have heard people say that the short game just deserts you when you haven't played for a while. The reason that it does, I believe, is that it depends on that feel or touch factor that we talked about in the last chapter. It is a rather nebulous thing, a sort of amalgam of the senses that relates control of fine movement, with timing of the strike and a deftness of touch that has all been unconsciously calculated by the brain as it strives to cause the body and limbs to impart the correct amount of force. As an occasional golfer it struck me that those pitches close to the green, especially if a hazard had to be cleared on the way, were extremely difficult. They often resulted in a mishit shot that scuttled across the green or a weak pitch into the hazard. It was very frustrating.

I suppose one of my problems when I started out was that I played with a half set of clubs. I remembered reading that Harry Vardon only ever used seven clubs, since he thought that was sufficient for all eventualities. Fool that I was, I somehow thought that if seven clubs were enough for Vardon, that was how the game should be played. The logic was that if you used fewer clubs then you had to become more adept with them and conjure shots up. Golfing geniuses like Seve Ballesteros did it all the time. Regular pros seemed able to bend balls one way or the other with any club in the bag. But what was I, one of the canaille thinking of? A lowly, occasional golfer could not expect to conjure up shots when he only played every few months and used a half set of out-of-date clubs.

Then I saw the light. Golf is an equipment sport. You are permitted to carry fourteen clubs and it is foolish to carry fewer than you need. I therefore started to carry the full set. Then I fell into the second common trap. I started to use the one club for virtually all shots from 50 yards in to the hole – that's right, the good old pitching wedge.

The trouble was that for the occasional golfer it is not easy to gauge those distances. Pros don't have the problems that we amateurs have because they know precisely how far they hit the ball with each club. You often hear of them selecting a particular club to land the ball in a particular spot to give themselves a full wedge shot in so that they can spin the ball, rather than having to manufacture a shot from a shorter distance. That is all very well when you can spin the ball or get it to stop almost dead; most golfers cannot. And then there is the slight difficulty of managing to hit the ball to a precise point that leaves you with an exact distance to the flag!

That is why I went back to basics and decided to devise a strategy which would allow me to develop some consistency in the 30-yard and inwards area. That is, I wanted to reduce my errors and increase my chances of being able to chip and single putt. My strategy is simply to use three clubs rather than one. This might not sound like rocket science, and I am sure that lots of people already do something similar, but the point is that it is a strategy that should help the occasional golfer who has not enough time to practice.

THREE CLUBS

Instead of even thinking of using a pitching wedge for these shots that are close to but not on the green, and which may be anything up to 30 or 40 yards away, I use a 5, 7 and 9 iron. My aim is to chip the ball onto the playing surface and let it run up to the hole. The occasional golfer may benefit from this approach, because you are dramatically reducing the reliance on feel or touch.

THE CHIP SHOT

I use a putting grip for this rather than the regular grip as the shot is more in keeping with a putt than regular play. I play it from the middle of the stance, shortening the grip so that I play it at the same length as my putter.

I hit the same shot with all three clubs, the aim being to chip the ball onto an area of the green and then allow it to run up to the hole.

5 iron – aim to land it a quarter of the way to the hole from where you play it and it should run up to the hole

7 iron – aim to land it a third of the way to the hole from where you play it and it should run up to the hole

9 iron – aim to land it half way to the hole from where you play it and it should run up to the hole

It is as simple as that. Those clubs work for me and I achieve better results than I did when I tried to pitch the ball up close. The elevation of the club will throw the ball up enough and it will land and continue its roll, thus you have less 'feeling' to do to get the ball close. It will work out mathematically, so to speak. And when you have a specific target to land the ball on you will dramatically reduce the risk of fluffing the shot, which is not uncommon when you try to finesse a pitch.

You must, of course, know how far you have to play the ball, so you do need to walk up and pace the distance to the flag. Then

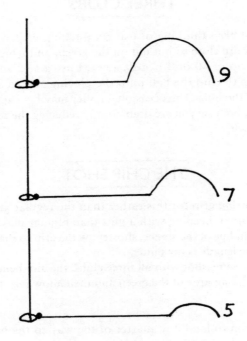

The three chipping clubs.

you quarter, third or halve the distance and choose the club that is going to do the job. Obviously, when you are on the green you assess if it is uphill or downhill and factor that in. Also decide whether you want to leave yourself an uphill or downhill put, so think about that too.

So, you pace it out, decide which club as you survey the green and you pick the landing area that you aim at. If you hit it you will be surprised at how the ball rolls out its distance to the flag.

This running-in was the method that was used frequently by the great players of the past. Johnny Farrell the 1928 US Open champion (he tied with Bobby Jones and beat him in a 36-hole play-off) regarded the chip shot as an 'elevated putt' useful from anywhere inside 40 yards.

For the occasional golfer like myself I highly recommend this method of approach.

14

GOLF PSYCHOLOGY

'Golf always makes me so damned angry.'
King George V (1865–1936)

In the Victorian age phrenology was very much in vogue. Phrenologists set up in consulting practice all over the country, rather like physicians, and were consulted by members of the public who wanted to have their character analysed or wanted to know what direction they should take in life. The theory behind it was that the lumps, bumps and prominences on the skull related to the contours of the brain. The phrenologists claimed thereby to be able to assess an individual's talents or deficiencies, or their strengths and weaknesses.

It has all been dismissed as pseudo-science, of course, since there is no correlation between the lumps on the head and the appearance of the brain. Certainly there does not appear to be any evidence that you can predict how the mind will work according to the shape of either the skull or the brain. However, for about a century and a half phrenology was held in high esteem by many people including Prime Minister William Gladstone who declared that as a system of mental philosophy it was far superior to any other system that anyone had proposed. The great inventor Thomas Alva Edison had been taken to a phrenologist and said that he had no idea that he had a talent for invention until he was told so by a practitioner of the art.

I have no doubt that if phrenology was resurrected as a means of helping people overcome the problems that they experience when they play golf, especially the angst caused in competitive play, phrenologists would be inundated with clients. Golf is a game that gets under people's skin; it plays with the mind and very often becomes an obsession. And many people have probably ended up

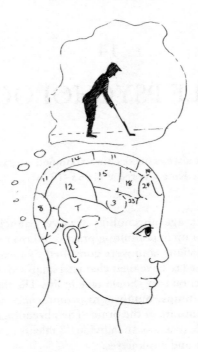

with lumps on their heads after playing what they perceive as a bad round of golf, as a result of bumping their heads against trees or wildly throwing their club skywards in frustration.

GOLF AND SUPERSTITION

My old golfing mate Glen Dullan used to be extremely superstitious when he played golf. He carried a lucky silver sixpence that he used as a golf marker (he had found it in a Christmas pudding). Then, on his first outing with it at a Boxing Day Texas scramble organised by some of the guys at the hospital golfing society, he won third prize. From then on he was convinced that his sixpence was a lucky one and he always used it to mark his ball. The fact that he never seemed to win anything again did not bother him – he had made up his mind and that was that. That happens a lot with surgeons.

Talking about coins used as markers, Jesper Parnevik apparently uses a coin but never marks a ball with the coin heads up. And even the great Jack Nicklaus is reputed to always carry three coins in his pocket to keep in the good books of the golfing gods.

THE MAGIC PLUS FOURS

P.G. Wodehouse wrote a wonderful golfing tale about a chap who was a golfing disaster, but then he discovered a ridiculous-looking pair of plus fours that he was convinced were magic. He wore them and his game was transformed as he worked his way through the club until he was well nigh unbeatable. But as he became better and in his mind invincible, so he underwent a personality change.

I shall say no more about the story for it is worth seeking out and reading, and I have no wish to spoil your fun by revealing more. I mention it also because it beautifully describes the effect that suggestion has on the mind.

I should add that I have no shares in any plus fours clothing company, and I personally wouldn't be seen dead in them. A kilt is a far better garment for playing golf, in my humble opinion.

GOLF CLOTHES

It has to be admitted, no matter how much you love golf, and no matter how liberal-minded you are, there is something about golfing attire. It is different to other sports. There is perhaps a smack of the outré about it, a little eccentricity even.

Without meaning to offend anyone, for people do have a living to make and many depend upon selling ranges of sports clothes, let me just say that you can usually tell when someone has been out playing golf. It is nothing to do with the bag; it is more to do with the checked trousers, the socks, garish shirts and the ubiquitous baseball hat or sun-visor. Having said all that many golfers have particular articles of clothing that they consider lucky. They might be shoes, socks, shirts, hats or even particular underwear. I knew one chap who always wore long johns under his trousers no matter what the weather was like.

I hasten to add that I only know this because they showed above his socks in the changing room.

Anyway, who are we lesser mortals to sneer at superstitions when Tiger Woods only wears a red shirt on the last day of a tournament? Is that a superstition? Apparently not, he has been heard to say that it is just like wearing a uniform. A habit rather than a belief.

THE RUB OF THE GREEN

You will hear this expression bandied around a lot. The rub of the greens means that golfers accept that they will have good luck and bad luck – some days you seem to get the good bounces and yet on other days if a ball can find a sprinkler cover to bounce on it will do so and skip over the green to end up plugged in a bunker. Perhaps that is why we develop these little superstitions. They can't do any real harm, can they, and when all is said and done they might actually work.

THE MOST IMPORTANT CLUB

This is another old golfing saying – the most important club is not the putter, not the driver, but the 'one between the ears', in other words the brain. It is probably quite true, because many golfers defeat themselves through negative thinking. That is not just the ordinary golfer but also some of the professional players at the upper echelons of the game. Why else do they seek, consult and even include sports psychologists on their payrolls, along with their caddie, their physiotherapist and their butler? It is because these latter-day phrenologists can help them smooth out those troublesome lumps and bumps or whatever else it is that causes their game to be less than perfect. There is a lot at stake, of course.

When that club between the ears is working well for you then all is truly well with the world – it is almost like playing in a state of Zen. The pros talk about being in the zone, when nothing distracts you, the swing works like clockwork and the hole seems like a bucket that you can't miss. Unfortunately those

days come less frequently than the days when the club between the ears just doesn't get going. In actual fact, it probably will be going, beating away like a metronome to your game's detriment.

To assess just how much the club between your ears works against you, you have only to think about your game. If you play off a handicap you will know the level that you can expect to play at on a day-to-day basis, yet even the high handicap player will shoot pars. Over several rounds he or she will probably par every hole on the course. So why can't they all be strung together? Is it ineptitude? No, it is probably much to do with expectation. You expect to fail. And if you hit a purple patch and shoot several pars together, you just know that the wheels are going to come off, to use another common golfing expression, and sure enough, you'll drive out of bounds, or into the stream or pond, and your putts will start to lip out.

A similar thing can happen when you think that you will play smartly and instead of reaching for the big driver to attempt the difficult carry you opt to take a 5 iron and go for a safety shot. The only thing is that you then bring a sapling into range, probably the only possible thing that could impede your next shot. What happens, bang – you strike the ball straight at it and it lodges behind it so that you are going to have to play out or risk further catastrophe. It is a curious phenomenon, but what it demonstrates is how well that club between the ears can do when it is swung with a negative thought in mind. Negative thinking will cause you to do the very thing you have tried to avoid.

LOGOTHERAPY AND ANTICIPATORY ANXIETY

I talked about expectation. On good days when you are fortunate enough to get in the zone you expect success, on other days you are more likely to get negative expectation. This is actually all to do with anticipatory fear. Let me get serious for a while because there are now things that are worth knowing about and considering, because they may help you deal with some of the negative thinking that is so common in golf.

I am going to tell you about the work of Dr Viktor Frankl. He was a holocaust survivor and the founder of a system of psychiatry known as 'logotherapy' (this is sometimes referred to as the 'Third Viennese School of Psychiatry', Sigmund Freud's Psychoanalysis being the first and Alfred Adler's Individual Psychology being the second). Frankl had developed his theories during stays in three different concentration camps, including the dreaded Auschwitz. He lost his family in the horrific conditions of the camps, yet he survived because he made it his aim to help others to survive by altering the way they thought. He clearly saved many people from suicide.

In establishing a philosophy that he called Logotherapy, meaning therapy based on wisdom or study, he established three basic beliefs. Firstly, that life has meaning under all circumstances, even the most miserable ones. Secondly, that our main motivation is our will to find meaning in life. Thirdly, that we have freedom to find meaning in what we do, and what we experience.

This might sound a bit heavy, but it has relevance to all areas of life, including our leisure activities such as golf. And of course if golf is more than a game in your life, then the anxieties you might associate with it assume greater importance in your mind. The essence of all this is that we have choice as to how we view things. One must work against a tendency to be pessimistic and to try to become an optimist.

SELF-TALK

To begin with, you have to consider self-talk. This is the name that we give to the endless stream of thoughts that run through your head every day. Pessimists tend to have a lot of negative automatic thoughts. Let me give you four examples. These may be quite foreign to optimists, but even if you are generally an optimist, in golf you may relate to some of this:

They magnify and filter. That is, they magnify the negative factors in a situation and filter out the positives. For example, a pessimist might complete ten tasks very well in a day, but one does not go so well. That is the one that preoccupies them and the others are filtered out and forgotten. The pessimistic golfer cannot forget the bad shots.

They personalise everything. A bad event is assumed to be their fault, because of something they may have done, or because someone has reacted against them. Something they have done caused the bad play that day.

They catastrophise everything. They only see the worst scenario. Because of that they may adopt avoidance behaviour. This may result in trying to avoid the hazard too much, so that you shoot right into it.

They only see in black or white, never in shades of grey. It is good or bad, more often bad than good.

But all this negative thinking can be changed. To do so you have to develop self-awareness and become aware of the 'self-talk' thought dialogue that takes place in your mind, but stop listening to the negative side. Just because bad things may have happened in the past does not mean that is how the future will be. The past is not the same as the future and there is no reason why it should be unless you allow it to be. Use your mind. Instead of thinking 'I can't do this,' think 'this is an opportunity to do well.' Instead of thinking 'uh-oh, there's that bunker I always go into,' tell yourself, 'there is no reason I'll go into it this time.'

And even if you do, so what!

FEAR AND EXCITEMENT

It is quite common to feel nervous when playing in competition, it is a natural reaction to the release of adrenaline from the adrenal glands. This speeds up the heart, quickens the breathing, causes the mouth to go dry and butterflies to erupt in the tummy. It is the body's way of getting you ready to either fight or fly away as quickly as possible. You can imagine that in days when such reactions were necessary in order to survive this reaction would have been very useful.

The way that you perceive this, however, can have an important bearing on the way that you perform on the course. If you perceive these feelings as being unpleasant then you will feel anxious. On the other hand if you can turn the way you perceive them into a pleasant sensation, then you will feel excited. The two sensations have the same adrenaline drive, and they can be turned to work for you. This is what top athletes and sportsmen do all the time – they use that heightened state positively to enhance performance rather than negatively to reduce or impair it.

The thing is that once you allow the adrenaline rush to make you feel fearful the mind takes off and enters a circuit of negative thinking. That is when you avoid going for the shot, play safe, and then hammer a shot straight at the hazard. You focus so much on the negative that you no longer see the positive.

Make the adrenaline work for you. Be excited; get that excited feeling to help you to hit the perfect shot that your partners are going to admire.

PARADOXICAL INTENTION

Viktor Frankl realised that much of the difficulty that we create for ourselves in so many areas of life is all to do with anticipatory anxiety. It is because we anticipate the event with fear that we get into more and more negative thinking. We do our utmost to avoid it. When you think about it, this happens when people have difficulty sleeping. They can get into a state about not getting to sleep that they try everything they can to get to sleep, including taking sleeping tablets from their doctor. They may work for a while, but then generally the dose has to be escalated and they may find that they can no longer cope without them.

To deal with this Frankl suggested that instead of trying to suppress the problem, you should face it. For the insomniac that instead of going to bed and trying to sleep, you should go to bed and try to stay awake for as long as possible. In most cases you can't do it and you fall asleep. In the act of trying to do the paradoxical thing, you remove the fear and the problem disappears.

LET'S GET PRACTICAL

I suspect that if you have read as far as this in this chapter, then you have read something which you can relate to. That being the case it means that you can also do something about some of these feelings that may be hampering your game.

GOLF IS ONLY A GAME

'Only a game?' I hear people exclaim. Well, yes I am afraid that it is only a game. Oh, I know that some matches are destined to go down in history as the greatest, the longest, the most nail-biting, and however else you like to describe them, yet don't get things out of proportion. Golf is not a war, it is not a conflict, it is not life-threatening and the security of the realm does not depend on it. It is a game and only a game. Yet for many golfers, golf matches cause them so much anxiety that they cannot sleep for nights beforehand. It assumes ever increasing importance. Why is that? Is it because one does not like to be defeated? Will losing that match diminish you as a human being? Does it really matter in the scheme of things?

The answer to these questions is actually 'no'. If you get excessively anxious about playing golf it is because you have allowed a mere game, a pastime, to assume too much importance. When that happens then you are liable to tighten the muscles, worry too much about the outcome and be unable to enjoy the game.

By diminishing the importance of the game, by telling yourself that it matters, but it doesn't matter a lot, you will be able to enjoy it a lot more. You will also find that by diminishing the anxiety around it, you will probably play better.

USE PARADOXICAL INTENTION

The whole point is that it is anxiety in anticipation of something that causes most trouble. That can be anxiety about something a long time ahead, such as an important tournament or championship, or something imminent, like the drive at the first tee, or the first putt to save a hole.

Worrying about something rarely produces any good effect, it is usually wasted energy. That is why diminishing the event's importance is such a good idea. If it is a tournament, then get it into your mind that it does not matter all that much. Golf is only a game. Get yourself thinking that you are going to enjoy it, not dread it.

For those immediate events, the thought causing the anxiety is not the shot that you have to make itself, it is the anxiety about the outcome – the outcome that you have in mind is usually failure.

Now this next bit might sound mad to you. Instead of going up to the shot like a bag of nerves worrying that you are going to make a mess of it and trying very hard not to make a mess of it, do the opposite. That's right, really, try the opposite. Go there, tell yourself it is just a game, it doesn't matter a great deal, and try and make a mess of it. You will almost inevitably relax and go and make a perfect stroke.

Once you challenge the bad thought the anxiety disappears – you stop trying not to make a mess and when you come to the actual stroke there is no anxiety, no tensing of muscles and the stroke will work.

Now I realise that you might find it hard to actually go out there and try that on a medal competition day, but do it when you are playing in a friendly. You will still get those moments when particular shots stress you, try it then. You will find that it works in the vast majority of cases.

Also, try to make yourself feel tense on certain shots. That is not what you usually do, but you will find it very hard to do. Imagine that each shot is potentially crucial in a major event. Gradually, the more you do it the more you will lose the anticipatory anxiety so that you can play better, more relaxed golf.

PICTURE THE SHOT

Good golfers do not address the ball without having a good mental picture of the shot that they are going to hit. In their mind they see the ball fly off in the right direction, with the right trajectory, and they do not even see the hazard. The less adept golfer does none of these things. The mental picture of the hazard, the danger, is all that he sees and the resultant swing is not properly computed by the brain. The point is that if you get the picture right in your mind then the club between your ears will get the club in your hands working correctly.

PLAYING IN FRONT OF PEOPLE

This causes a lot of golfers problems. They imagine that other golfers are watching them, scrutinising their swing or their putting technique and inwardly criticising. This causes them anxiety and they perform poorly as a result.

Here are two ways of dealing with this. Firstly, stop putting yourself at the centre of the universe. The other players are there to play golf, they are really not that bothered about how your swing looks. They are just watching and waiting for you to do what you have to so that they can then focus on what matters to them – their own shot. It does not matter what your swing looks like.

Playing in front of people is easy.

The other thing is to go completely the other way and consider yourself to be an actor. You act the great golfer, imagining that you are playing the part of Vardon, Nicklaus or Woods in a movie. You take on their skill and you revel in the limelight. You want your partner or opponent to watch your gold-plated swing and deft putting touch.

HITTING OVER A HAZARD

Some golfers will do anything to avoid having to hit over a hazard, even playing a sort of zigzag game around it. Forget that, play sensible strategic golf, but don't allow yourself to become afraid of a shot because you have to play along the side of, or over a hazard. Enjoy yourself. You can make the shot. The anticipatory anxiety is liable to become self-prophetic otherwise and it makes you play the weak shot into the hazard.

You should tell yourself that it doesn't matter. There is nothing to be afraid of, you can make the shot.

Your imagination tends to increase the significance of the hazard but use your imagination to ignore it. Know how far the ball has to travel, pick your spot and shoot. What is the big deal if it goes in the hazard anyway?

WEAK CHIP INTO THE BUNKER

This is essentially the same. You walk up to the greenside bunker that you have to chip over to land on the green. What happens? Your mind shows you hitting it too weakly straight into the hazard. The reason is that you get afraid of hitting it and when that happens you ease off and try to baby it onto the green. Your mind is trying to do a finesse shot that just clears the bunker and allows the ball to trickle up to the hole.

It is the wrong strategy for one thing. You should be aiming above all to clear the hazard – it doesn't matter if you go past the flag, you can putt back. But if you go in the sand you have to play out and then putt.

There is nothing to be afraid of. Hit the ball with the club, and it will lift the ball up and well over. You know you can do it.

USE COLOURS

It is not a bad idea to use colours to help you. Choose a colour that you find exciting, and with a pen of that colour draw a spot on your golf glove, so that you see it when you take up your stance. Think of the colour, red for example, and feel excited. Use that excited feeling to enjoy the game, because when you are enjoying it you will relax and give yourself the best chance of playing well.

If you need to be relaxed then choose a relaxing colour, a colour you associate with a relaxed image from somewhere or sometime in your life. Ink that colour on your glove. Focus on it as you take your stance. Relax and enjoy the game and you will play well.

These are excellent little links that you can make and the beauty is that they work.

NOT UP, NOT IN

This old adage makes great sense, but so many people make life hard on the greens for themselves by absorbing that other old adage, 'if you have two putts for it, use them'. They are also told to lag putt, meaning aim that first putt to stop within 2 or 3ft of the hole. Then very often they then end up putting 4 or even 6ft short. Then they wonder why they did that.

The reason is simple, they allowed their mind to think that the target is the great circle two or three feet across that has the hole at its centre. They are told to aim at a bucket rather than the hole; in so doing the mind computes that it does not have to instruct the body to hit the ball to reach the hole, but the circumference of the imaginary 'bucket'. The result is that the ball is struck so weakly that it lands 2ft short of the circumference which itself is 2ft from the hole.

Instead of using a large target centred on the hole, make just the centre of the hole the target. I mentioned in the putting chapter that practicing putting to a golf tee instead of a hole is a good idea. Indeed, if that is your target rather than a hole you will improve your putting. And if a hole is your target rather than that imaginary bucket you are more likely to reach it.

FORGET THE LAST SHOT
OR THE LAST HOLE

Letting go is something that a lot of golfers find difficult to do. They play a bad shot, or they hit a decent shot and an unlucky bounce causes the ball to end up out of bounds, in a hazard or in an awkward lie. Anger results and a swipe is made at the next shot, with the expected result.

Really, it is not worth getting in a stew about it. You just need to dust your hands and get on with the next shot as if the last one hadn't happened. You then make a good stroke.

15

GOLFING MALADIES

'I find the medicine worse than the malady.'
John Fletcher (1579–1625),
English dramatist

Doctors are well advised to pretend to be plumbers or accountants when they go a-golfing. If not, they are likely to hear about their opponent's latest medical condition by the second green. By the sixth they will have heard their entire past medical history and by the ninth it is rare not to have had a run through about their bowel habit. The course does not actually lend itself to physical examinations, but the locker room is a common place for medical consultations and the 19th hole, when one is longing for half a pint of bitter, can be more like a waiting room than the waiting room that you have just escaped from for the afternoon.

The truth is that golf is a game that causes more than its fair share of ailments. For many the best medicine is simply to give up the game, but not many folk want to do that.

THE YIPS

This condition has actually been responsible for more golfers giving up the game than any other. It is a state in which fine movements are difficult to control and tends only to occur in putting. The name was actually given to it by the great Tommy Armour, who won three majors, but who suffered the golfing woe of the putting twitch.

Effectively the golfer with the yips becomes aware of a twitching as they address the ball. The small muscles of the wrists seem to go into spasm and jab at the ball. Sometimes the ball may be hit repeatedly in a series of movement hiccups, each of which counts as a stroke. It seems to be worse the nearer to the hole one gets.

The condition is most common in people who have been playing for a long time and it affects around a third of golfers who have been playing for 25 years or more. It is in fact a bit of a rag-bag term, rather than a proper medical one. It may be simple nerves in some people, whereas in others it is a definite focal dystonia, or movement disorder.

The two most beneficial things that a golfer afflicted with the yips can do is firstly to use their breath properly. Become aware of breathing in and out before taking the putt. Stand over the putt and focus on two or three inhalations and exhalations. Aim to feel the smooth flow of air. Focus on the putt, take another deep inhalation and as you start the exhalation begin the putt, make the stroke and keep going through the ball and stop.

Secondly, you may find that you need to completely change the pattern of your putting stroke. Changing the putting grip, perhaps even reversing the position of the hands in what is called a cross-handed grip, will often help. The aim is to remove the usual muscle movements and changing the putting stroke entirely can work wonders, to the point even where a right-hander can putt left-handed and a left-hander might try going right-handed.

'Next!'

GOLFER'S BACK PAIN

Golf involves walking and striking a ball around a golf course. There are 18 holes and depending upon your level you can expect to strike the ball anywhere between 72 and 110 times. For most of these shots you will actually have to strike the stationary ball hard which means that you have to perform a swing resulting in you entering a hitting zone many times in the course of a round. Many people who play golf have back problems from this one-sided hitting. That does not mean that you should avoid it, just be careful. You are better playing on a course, walking between shots rather than standing and striking a hundred balls on the range or the practice ground.

Both the neck and the lower back tend to be the areas that golfers develop pains in. The problem is that it is a one-sided sport and the more you play the more you have attempted to groove your golf swing. You should, therefore, try to balance it by also doing other activities which are two-sided, like walking, swimming or riding a bike.

GOLFER'S ELBOW

This is actually called 'medial epicondylitis'. It is an inflammation on the epicondyle, the inner bony prominence on the elbow, where the flexor muscles of the arm are anchored. Their purpose is to flex the wrist and close the hand. You can see, therefore how it may occur in golf.

In actual fact this is not seen any more frequently in golf than in other sports. It is just called that, in the same way that tennis elbow, the same pain on the outer surface of the elbow, is associated with tennis.

They do necessitate rest for a while and if they persist then a doctor or physiotherapist should be consulted. A steroid injection might help, as may acupuncture.

SORE KNEES AND FLAT FEET

Painful knees are common in golf, which is not surprising when you think of the lateral movements and twisting forces that are applied to them during a golf swing. Part of the problem can relate to the position that a golfer tends to get his or her feet into. The traditional teaching is to buttress the weight change against the inner surface of the back foot. This effectively means making the feet flatter during the stroke. The thing is that the movement, which we call pronation, whereby you turn the foot inwards, will throw a strain on the inner surface of the knees. This has actually been demonstrated by researchers in Sweden using MRI scans on a large group of people.

If you have a tendency to be flat-footed then you may be at risk of golfer's knee pain. To see if you have flat feet just stand with your wet feet after a shower or bath. If you are flat footed you will leave a whole footprint on the floor. If you are not you will not leave an inner imprint.

If you are flat-footed, see a podiatrist about getting some implants to put into your golf shoes. It may save you a lot of pain.

GOLFER'S HEEL

This is also called policeman's heel. It is a painful inflammatory condition affecting the under surface of the heel, so that walking can become painful and standing can be a trial. Its proper name is 'plantar fasciitis' and the under surface of the heel becomes very tender and one or two spots will be exquisitely tender. Rest is needed and the application of ice may help.

Probably the best thing that one can do to prevent it is to get into the habit of incorporating calf-stretching into your day. Simply stand about a yard from a wall with the soles of your feet kept flat on the ground, then rest your hands flat against the wall and do a few (5 or 6) gentle press-ups against the wall. Do this two or three times a day. Try also rotating your ankles and wiggling your toes whenever you sit down to eat or watch TV.

If it doesn't settle then see a doctor, because sometimes a steroid injection may be needed to relieve it. Acupuncture may also help.

DON'T GIVE UP GOLF

The thing is that golf is actually good for you. Research from Sweden looked at the physical demands on middle-aged golfers during a round. They found that the exercise intensity ranged from 40 to 70 per cent of maximum aerobic power, despite the short walk, stop and hit a shot pattern of the sport. To put that into perspective, a 4-hour round of golf has the same benefit as a 45-minute fitness class. For many middle-aged and elderly people a round of golf is probably a better way of getting the exercise, and it adds interest to the walking.

Another study from Hawaii analysed data on men aged between 71 and 93 years of age. They found that the risk of heart disease decreased by 15 per cent for each half mile walked daily. More than that, they found that men who walked one and a half miles or more per day had less than half the rate of heart disease of the men who walked less than a quarter of a mile.

Yet another ongoing research study on the benefits of walking has been going on at Stanford University in California since the 1960s. The consistent finding is that the death rate is lower as physical activity increases. The risk of death drops 21 per cent as walking distance increases from fewer than 3 to 9 or more miles a week.

If you compare playing golf with a golf cart with golf when you walk the course, it has been found that you burn 2.5 to 3.7 calories per minute when you use a cart, whereas if you golf-walk you burn between 5 and 8 calories per minute. Very interestingly, although you would think that carrying your bag or pulling a trolley would be even better for you; this does not seem to be the case. The benefit seems to be in the process of walking, not in expending energy hauling the bag or trolley. If you do like to carry your own bag, or like to haul a trolley, be sure to swap the sides that you carry the bag with, or the hand that you pull your bag.

16

SCORING

'Rara avis in terris nigroque simillima cygno'
('a rare bird in the lands, and very like a black swan')
Juvenal (first century AD),
Roman poet

Golf is a fun game when you are scoring well, but it can be purgatory when you are playing miserably and scoring badly. You can get absolutely trounced by a better player, which is not a lot of fun. To combat all of that golf is fairly unique among sports with its handicap system which permits an absolute duffer to play with a really good golfer and have an even match.

Of course, because the handicap system is hierarchical, a player with a low handicap may feel a cut above the golfer with a high handicap. At club level members are divided into Tigers and Rabbits. They can play with each other and be perfectly sociable, yet who knows what emotions may be simmering away as the scores are added up.

THOSE QUAINT NAMES

To the golfer the names given to the scores that one may get on a hole are things of charm. For the non-golfer they are simply odd labels used in a decidedly odd sport. In the old days there were no such names. The winning of a hole was simply achieved by taking fewer shots than your opponent. The winner was the player who won the most holes over the course of the round. The actual total number of shots taken only came later.

BOGEY OR PAR

In 1890 Hugh Rotherham of the Coventry Golf Club introduced the idea that there should be a standard score for each hole on the course, which a hypothetical perfect golfer playing perfect golf on each hole would be able to achieve. This score was called the ground score.

A year later Dr Thomas Browne, the honorary secretary at Great Yarmouth Golf Club, introduced this concept to his club. The idea of the hypothetical perfect golfer caused some amusement and one of his friends remarked that he must be a real bogey man. Dr Browne then called the ground score the bogey score. Soon all clubs adopted it as the normal term and it was effectively the score that we now call par.

The term par actually derived from the stock market where a commodity would have its fixed value, or par, but its price could fluctuate above or below its par.

In America the bogey came to be regarded as a score above the par, and eventually the rest of the world followed suit. So par became the number of strokes that a hole should be completed in, and a bogey was one above it, a double bogey was two above and so on.

EVER RARER BIRDS

Getting below par on holes was not something that average players did very often, so bird names were introduced. As players started to achieve ever more remarkable results a series of even rarer birds were used.

Birdie – 1 under par

Eagle – 2 under par

Albatross – 3 under par

Condor – 4 under par

Ostrich – 5 under par

Ever rarer birds.

Condors are extremely rare birds, but four have actually been achieved:

Larry Bruce holed a dogleg par 5 at Hope Country Club in Arkansas in 1962.

Shaun Lynch holed a dogleg par 5 at Teign Valley Golf Club in Devon in 1995.

Mike Crean hit a colossal straight drive into the hole at Green Valley Ranch Golf Club in Denver, Colorado, in 2002. It is said that wind assistance and high altitude must have had something to do with it.

Jack Bartlett holed a par 5 at the Royal Wentworth Falls Country Club in 2007.

An ostrich is theoretical of course, but one day, who knows?

LESS RARE BIRDS AND STUFF

Far more common than the regal birds found below par are the birds or things that plague players when they score above par on a hole.

Bogey – 1 over par. And double, triple, etc.

Buzzard – a double bogey

Snow White – 7 (as in Snow White and the Seven Dwarfs)

Snowman – 8 (as per the shape of an 8)

Tadpole – 9 (as per the shape of a 9)

Hen – 10

Archaeopteryx – 15 or more over par, as achieved by the great Tommy Armour who once took a 23 at a par 5, 18 over par.

HANDICAP AND STROKE INDEX

The system by which golfers are graded is called the handicap. Effectively a handicap is a means of getting a head start. A player who can play the whole round to par would receive a 0 handicap and be called a scratch golfer. Professional golfers have no handicaps.

A 2 handicap would subtract 2 shots from his score and an 18 handicap would subtract 18.

Each hole on the course is given a stroke index. The hardest hole on the course would be stroke index 1 and the easiest would be stroke index 18. In matchplay our 2 handicap player receives strokes at holes with stroke index 1 and 2, whereas the 18 handicap would receive a stroke on each hole. A 10 handicap player would receive strokes on holes with stroke index up to and including 10.

In the UK the maximum handicap for men is 28, for women is 36 and for juniors is up to 54.

17

SO WHAT DO YOU WANT TO PLAY?

'Don't play too much golf. Two rounds a day are plenty.'
Harry Vardon (1870–1937),
six times Open champion

The first types of games were matchplay. It took a while before players began determining a game on the basis of total number of strokes taken. Perhaps this reflected the differing numbers of holes on various courses, the differing lengths of holes and the varying difficulty of courses. Remember that in the early days courses were played over heath, moor and pasture, without the benefit of fairways being neatly trimmed or greens in the sense that we now have them. And of course there was the stymie.

THE STYMIE

Everyone has heard the expression, 'to be stymied'. It means to be impeded or to be prevented from doing something – a problem has to be overcome before one can move on. It comes from golf and referred to a situation on the green when one player's ball was directly between the hole and the other player's ball. If the balls were 6in or less apart the obstructing ball could be lifted to allow the other to putt. If the balls were more than 6in apart then the furthest player had to attempt to spin his ball round the other or chip it over. The latter was called 'lofting a stymie'. If the obstructing ball was hit the player who had struck the shot had to play his next putt from where it landed up. If he knocked

Lofting a stymie.

the obstructing ball into the hole, then the obstructing ball was considered holed, without having to count an extra putt.

Understandably, all manner of gamesmanship was possible, and the stymie was taken out of the game in 1952 on the agreement of both the R&A and the USGA.

MATCHPLAY

This is the format often played in amateur matches either between individuals or teams. Each hole is played for and can either be won or halved, if the players take the same number of strokes, taking handicaps into consideration if applicable.

STROKEPLAY

This is the format played in most professional tournaments, where there is no handicap. It is the usual format in club medal competitions.

Each player completes the whole round, playing every shot. At the end the gross score has the player's handicap subtracted to give the nett score. The player with the lowest nett score wins.

FOUR BALL

This is a match between two teams, with two players on each team. Each player uses their own ball and the best score from each team counts. It can be played in either matchplay or strokeplay formats.

FOURSOME

Again, two teams with two players on each team. Here each team plays with only one ball, the two players taking alternate shots. It can be played in matchplay or strokeplay format. One player on each side will tee off on even holes and the other on odd holes.

GREENSOME

This is a variant of the foursome where each player on the team drives and then between them they decide which is the best drive. From then on they play alternate shots.

STABLEFORD

This very popular type of match was the brainchild of Dr Frank Barney Gorton Stableford (1870–1959). He was a member of the Wallasey Golf Club and also Royal Liverpool, and he was a surgeon and a highly accomplished golfer with a handicap of plus 1. The course at Wallasey is not an easy one, because when the wind howls the par fours can be extremely difficult to reach in regulation figures. It was while playing one day that he had the idea of devising a system which would enable players to continue to enjoy a game even if they had a few bad holes. Up until then players often tore scorecards up if they had played themselves out of contention.

In 1931 he invented the system that is forever associated with his name and a year later the first Stableford Competition was played at Wallasey Golf Club.

A Stableford is played off handicap. Each hole is played and a player can accrue the following points (when handicap is taken into account) on each hole:

Double bogey or more	0
Bogey	1
Par	2
Birdie	3
Eagle	4
Albatross	5
Condor	6

Thus a player receiving 2 shots on a hole, which a high handicapper with a handicap of greater than 18 will do on designated holes, could get a par which would convert into an eagle and he would score 4 points. If he had a gross eagle (3) on a par 5, his two shots would convert that into a 1 on a par five, so he would score 6 points.

It really is one of the best and most fun types of golf at club level and it has an added benefit in that it can speed up play. If a player can do no better than a double bogey he can pick his ball up and just record no score for that hole.

TEXAS SCRAMBLE

This is a fun type of golf in which teams (of two, three or four players) play. The whole team tee off together and then the best drive is selected. The other players pick up their balls and then they all play a second shot from the same place as the best drive.

They then select the best second shot and again they all play the third from there and select the best shot until the hole is finished. The team with the lowest score wins.

FLAG COMPETITION

This is another fun event in golf clubs where each player is given his or her handicap allowance which is added to the par for the course. They then have that number of strokes to see how far round the course they can go, planting a flag at the furthest point they reach with their allocation. That can, of course be less than the round if one is having a bad round, or it may extend well beyond the eighteenth and the player continues from the first.

MULLIGANS

This is not an official golf game but is often played in friendly matches with chums. A mulligan is when a player is allowed to play a shot again. There are no hard and fast rules of mulligans, but it is usual to allow a mulligan only on a tee shot. There is usually a limit to how many, often just one per nine holes, but sometimes if players are in a fun match for charity they may buy up to three mulligans. Another variant is to allow the same number of mulligans in a round as one's handicap.

18

ETIQUETTE

'If your opponent is playing several shots in vain attempts to extricate himself from a bunker, do not stand near him and audibly count his strokes. It would be justifiable homicide if he wound up his pitiable exhibition by applying his niblick to your head.'
Harry Vardon

In former times 'etiquette' specified a ticket that was tied to the necks of bags and parcels indicating their contents, so that they would be passed unchallenged as they were transported by coach, train and by sea. Over time it became associated with the behaviour that was expected in various areas of life. In the modern day many of these social codes have fallen by the wayside. Not so in golf, a sport that has always prided itself on its code of etiquette.

RESPECT YOUR OPPONENT

That doesn't mean that you have to fawn over him or her but you should:

be polite

arrive at the course in good time, so that you can pay your fee if needed, organise tees and have time for a little practice. Meet your opponent in good time ahead of your tee time

be quiet when he or she takes a shot

After you!

don't stride off if he or she can't find their ball

compliment him or her on good shots

don't offer advice on what's wrong with his or her game, unless you are asked for it

remember to play in order. You should drive according to who has the honour and you should play your shot when it is your turn. Furthest from the hole generally plays first and you should not rush up to your ball and hit it. The principle is that the player furthest from the hole plays first.

OBSERVE THE DRESS CODE

You may have a casual attitude to dress, but many golf clubs do not. They may be quite traditional and unless you observe their code you may not be allowed on the course. It is always as well to check with the professional by phone even before going to the course.

Jeans are generally frowned upon and t-shirts may not be permitted.

HAVE THE CORRECT EQUIPMENT

This means having a bag and a set of clubs. Five of you should not arrive at a course and expect to play together, sharing clubs from one or two bags.

You should also have appropriate golf shoes, only use a caddy car or caddy cart if permitted to do so and above all, have enough balls!

ON THE COURSE

You are there to have fun, but you should not impede other players in their enjoyment. Most clubs do not expect players to:

Wander round with cans or bottles of beer in their hands

Use mobile phones. Indeed on many courses this is verboten, no matter how big a hot-shot businessman you are

Shout, swear or make a lot of noise. Remember you can put other players off when they are concentrating on a shot. You should not press the players ahead or shout

Never play a shot when the players ahead are within range, no matter how inept you think you are. You may hit a scorcher and you could do someone an injury

Play slowly. That doesn't mean that you should run round, but you should play at a decent pace, not allowing your game to hold others up. The rule of thumb is that if your game falls more than one hole behind the players ahead, you should let the players behind play through

You should always replace divots

In bunkers, generally enter from behind the ball at the nearest point

Always use the rake to smooth the sand afterwards

ON THE GREEN

Leave your bag beyond the fringe and never lay it on the green

Do not practice on the greens

Repair pitch marks as you approach your ball

Avoid walking on a player's line

Offer to hold the flag when your opponent is about to putt and ask whether he or she wants it held or attending. If they want it attending that means that if the ball looks as if it is going to fall into the hole you should remove the flag.

Be quiet while your opponent putts

When you putt into the hole retrieve your ball straight away

Vacate the green promptly. It is not the time to mark your card

THE 19TH HOLE

Most rounds finish at the 19th hole, the usual name for the clubhouse bar. You should be aware that the clubhouse will probably have its own dress code. In some clubs there is a different dress code in the day and the evening. Some clubs have a spike bar, in that they allow golf shoes to be worn. Never assume this to be the case – it is always as well to use the locker room and change into appropriate clothing.

The 19th hole.

Two things to be aware of: firstly, the captain's chair. In many clubs it is forbidden for anyone except the captain to sit in it and the penalty is usually to buy drinks for everyone present. Secondly, if you have just had a hole-in-one, be careful of announcing it when you enter the bar. Again, buying a round of drinks is expected.

GAMESMANSHIP

The above are basically the dos and don'ts that you should consider. There are more, but they are enough to be going on with and it does the experienced golfer no harm to reflect upon how many of them he or she observes.

Unfortunately, it has to be said that not everyone plays by the rules. Some people cheat at golf, but in the end they only cheat themselves. Anyone caught cheating is liable to become a pariah at a club and may even be asked to leave.

To pretend that you are better than you are is a foolish thing to do, since your game will soon expose the truth. Similarly, many clubs have people who protect their handicaps, in that they maintain a higher handicap than they actually need in order to go pot-hunting. Of course, if the handicap system is working properly their handicap should reflect their performance.

In the bad old days it was not unknown for players holding dual membership of clubs to be able to hold different handicaps. That allowed such bandits to enter a competition and give the higher handicap but nowadays that should not happen.

Gamesmanship is not strictly speaking the same thing as cheating. It is when a player plays within the rules yet exerts pressure either in a subtle or unsubtle manner to put his or her opponent off a shot or off their game. Such things as coughing or lighting a pipe at the moment when someone is about to drive or putt are annoying, but commonplace. Directing someone's attention towards a hazard or remarking about the difficulty or otherwise of a shot may have a devastating effect on one's opponent.

But I am not going to say any more than that, because it isn't proper golf.

NAKED GAMESMANSHIP

Howard Hughes was a golfer who could cut corners, not necessarily by hitting the ball over hazards to take the direct line to the green, but rather by being in the position of having enough wealth to buy an advantage.

On one important needle game, upon which he had a tidy bet going, he hired a number of Hollywood starlets who popped up at various points of the match stark naked. It apparently distracted his opponent sufficiently for Hughes to win the match and the wager. Call that gamesmanship if you will.

WIND

At a tournament in 1959 the irascible golfer Tommy Bolt passed wind while his opponent was about to putt. He was fined a substantial amount of money for the act that was thought to have been a deliberate attempt to put the other player off.

THE RULES OF GOLF

Just as golf has always prided itself on its etiquette, so do golfers by and large obey the rules.

The original Rules of Golf were set down before the first ever competition at Leith by the Honourable Company of Edinburgh Golfers. They were relatively simple. Indeed, there were only thirteen rules.

1. You must Tee your Ball within a Club's length of the Hole.
2. Your Tee must be upon the Ground.
3. You are not to change the Ball which you Strike off the Tee.
4. You are not to remove Stones, Bones or any Break Club, for the sake of playing your Ball, Except upon the fair Green and that only within a Club's length of your Ball.
5. If your Ball comes among watter, or any wattery filth, you are at liberty to take out your Ball & bringing it behind the hazard and Teeing it, you may play it with any Club and allow your Adversary a Stroke for so getting out your Ball.
6. If your Balls be found any where touching one another, You are to lift the first Ball, till you play the last.
7. At Holling, you are to play your Ball honestly for the Hole, and not to play upon your Adversary's Ball, not lying in your way to the Hole.
8. If you should lose your Ball, by it's being taken up, or any other way, you are to go back to the Spot, where you struck last, & drop another Ball, And allow your adversary a Stroke for the misfortune.

9. No man at Holling his Ball, is to be allowed, to mark his way to the Hole with his Club, or anything else.

10. If a Ball be stopp'd by any Person, Horse, Dog or anything else, The Ball so stop'd must be play'd where it lyes.

11. If you draw your Club in Order to Strike, & proceed so far in the Stroke as to be bringing down your Club; If then, your Club shall break, in any way, it is to be Accounted a Stroke.

12. He whose Ball lyes farthest from the Hole is obliged to play first.

13. Neither Trench, Ditch or Dyke, made for the preservation of the Links, nor the Scholar's Holes, or the Soldier's Lines, Shall be accounted a Hazard; But the Ball is to be taken out teed /and play'd with any Iron Club.

John Rattray, Capt

The original rules as written above were only rediscovered in 1937, when a minute book of the Honourable Company of Edinburgh Golfers was examined. John Rattray was the captain of the club and the winner of their first competition.

The R&A published the first national set of rules in 1899.

The USGA was formed in 1894 and adopted the R&A rules when they came out in 1899. The two organisations operated independently, the USGA overseeing the rules in the USA and Mexico and the R&A doing the same in the UK and the rest of the world. From 1952 they have worked together.

The modern rules can be quite complex and it may pay the golfer to keep a set of them in their golf bag.

AND LAST OF ALL – THE WAGGLE

And so, gentle reader, we come to the end of the book. I hope that you may have found some interest in it. Perhaps you have found some facts that you were unaware of, or picked up an anecdote or two that amused you.

I was wondering about writing something that would finish the book off well. Maybe some swing idea that could be useful – something like imagining that you are a waiter and that on the backswing you need to get your right hand into a position as if you were holding a tray on which a glass of champagne was balanced. I was given that little snippet of advice once and it worked for me. Yet it may not work for everyone, since of course not everyone has worked as a waiter, and you may not care for champagne.

Then I thought perhaps something for the start of the swing would be more useful. And of course, that is it – *the waggle* – that is the name for those preliminary little back and forth movements that precede the swing. To the uninitiated they may seem superfluous nervous twitches preparatory to launching oneself at the ball. It should be anything but that.

The great Tommy Armour has a short chapter on it in his book *How To Play Your Best Golf All The Time*. He says that he was once told by George Duncan that a player will swing as he waggles. Tommy Armour took this on board and confirmed it through years of observation. The waggle is in fact a golf swing in miniature and you can predict the whole character of a golfer's game by the way he waggles. He therefore advised that a golfer should cultivate a smooth waggle, for it is as the old Scots saying goes, 'As ye waggle so shall ye swing.'

And so, I wish each and every golfer a happy, smooth waggle and continued enjoyment of this great game.

GLOSSARY

ace – hole in one
address – the position taken up just prior to striking the ball
albatross – 3 under par on a hole
amateur – someone who does not play for a living. Many
    amateurs play for money, so beware
approach – a shot to the green
archaeopteryx – 15 or more over par on a hole
back nine – the second 9
backswing – the first part of the swing away from the ball,
    before the downswing
baffie – old name for an approaching wood. More correctly a
    baffing spoon. It is probably equivalent to a 5 or 6 wood
bandit – someone who plays a mean game and who may profess
    to be less adept than they are
birdie – one under par on a hole
blind shot – a shot when you cannot see the flag
bogey – one over par on a hole
borrow – the curve that you see between the ball and the hole
    on the green
bunker – a depression in the course filled with sand. It is called
    a sand trap in the USA. It is a hazard and as such the club
    may not be grounded before playing the stroke, otherwise a
    2-point penalty is incurred
block – a shot that flies straight right of the target
break – another word for borrow
caddie – the person who carries the clubs. It comes from the
    French *cadet*
carry – the distance that the ball has to be flown through the air
    over a hazard or to reach fairway or green
casual water – a collection of water as in a puddle
chip – a short shot to the flag

cleek – an old club like a 3 iron

closed face– this is a position at address, when the club face is pointed to the left of the target (for a right-handed golfer)

closed stance – the left foot is further forward than the right (back) foot (for a right-handed golfer)

concede – to give an opponent a putt if it is so close that they cannot miss, or a hole if you are unable to do better than them

cross-handed grip – when the positions of the hands are reversed, with the left hand lower than the right for a right-handed player

cut – in a tournament a score that will demarcate where the field will be reduced. It usually takes place after 36 holes

cut shot – a shot that curves from left to right for a right-handed player

deuce – a 2

dimple – a depression in a golf ball

divot – a piece of turf removed when the ball is struck. A good golfer always replaces his or her divots

dogleg – a bend in a golf hole, so that the flag cannot be seen from the tee

down – means that one person is losing

draw – a shot that curves right to left for a right-handed player

drop – when a player is either given relief and permitted to drop the ball back into play. Depending on circumstances a penalty may or may not be incurred

eagle – 2 under par on a hole

etiquette – the code of behaviour

fade – a shot that travels left to right for a right-handed player

featherie – old ball consisting of a leather cover stuffed with boiled down feathers

flag – the flag atop the pin, which marks the position of the hole

fore! – a warning shout – '(look out be-)*fore!*'

green – the putting surface of very short grass

grounding – laying the club down on the ground behind the ball prior to the stroke. It is permitted anywhere except in a hazard

handicap – the system of evening out players according to their ability, so that good and less adept players can have a competitive game together hazard – a ditch, stream, pond or bunker that is an integral part of the course. The club may not be grounded before playing the shot, or a 2-stroke penalty ensues

hosel – the point where the shaft of the club continues into the clubhead

hook – a shot that bananas from right to left. A vicious one is called a duck-hook

lag – to putt up to the hole without seriously aiming to get it in

lateral hazard – a ditch or stream parallel to the fairway. It is usually well demarcated

links – a traditional seaside course

marker – a small disc or coin used to mark the ball on the green

mashie – old name for a mid iron. About a 5 iron

mashie-niblick – old name for an approaching iron, about a 7 iron

medal – usual club competition every month or mid-week

metal wood – a crazy term for a metal club that is equivalent to the old driver, brassie or spoon, or driver, 2 wood or 3 wood

nett – the score after handicap has been allowed for

open face – when the club face is aimed right of the target (for a right-handed golfer)

open stance – when the leading foot is behind the back foot (for a right-handed golfer)

out of bounds – anywhere outside the course. To play a shot out of bounds will incur a penalty shot and the shot must be retaken from the same point. Hence the player loses stroke and distance

pin – the pole that marks the position of the hole

pitch – a short approach shot played high to land and stop quickly or even with some backspin

play-off – in a competition if there is a tie then more holes or even a whole round will be played to decide the winner. The format varies tournament to tournament

push – a ball struck straight out to the right

rabbit – a high handicap player

read – the process of assessing the contours and speed of a green

rough – the long uncut grass beside the fairway

scratch – an excellent golfer who plays par golf

shank – a miss when the hosel of the club strikes the ball, causing it to fly off erratically, usually to the right sky – a mishit ball that shoots straight up, when the club gets right under the ball

slice – a ball that starts left and then rapidly moves right for a right-handed golfer

Vardon grip – the name for the overlapping grip

waggle – the back and forth movement before the actual stroke, as the player settles into their rhythm

Yips – the destructive movement problem that afflicts many golfers on the greens

ACKNOWLEDGEMENTS

Writing this book has been a great delight, if for no other reason than it has given me a quite legitimate reason to leave my study, pick up my bag of clubs and head off to the links on a regular basis. Ah, the bliss of research! Yet there are several people that I must thank for their parts in bringing this modest little volume to public view. Firstly, I thank Isabel Atherton, my fantastic agent who first suggested that I

should stop talking about golf and organise my thoughts into a book. Her advice has been greatly valued, as always.

Michelle Tilling, the commissioning editor at The History Press, kindly read through the book proposal and took it on board. I thank her for giving me a genuine reason to play more golf and to read more golf books and watch more golf movies.

Richard Leatherdale, my editor, helped to get the book into proper reading condition, for which I am grateful. If he ever gives up editing, I am sure he would make an excellent greenkeeper.

Fiona McDonald performed a sterling job in transforming my illustration ideas into actual line drawings. It has been a joy to work with her on this, our second book for The History Press.

Finally, thanks to my wife Rachel for listening to my endless anecdotes and reports of my adventures on the links while researching and writing this book – at least I think she was listening!